From Tattersalls To Triumphs

All proceeds from this book will be donated equally to the Retraining Of Racehorses and the Injured Jockeys Fund charities.

Michael Madden

The sport of horseracing has its own unique vocabulary, and for those not familiar with this I have included many of the frequently used terms in a glossary at the back of the book. The glossary is based upon my own understanding and things that I have learnt over the past twelve months. If you find any inaccuracies, or there are any terms that you think would be a useful inclusion, please let me know, and I will be sure to add them to any future publications.

Cover photograph by kind permission Mark Moon
Author photograph by kind permission Fiona Higginbotham

Copyright © 2022 by Michael Madden
All rights reserved. No part of this book may be reproduced, scanned, or distributed in any printed or electronic form without permission.

Foreword

I began writing this book in May 2022. At that time, Star Of Lady M had won two out of three, and Emerald Duchess had run twice disappointingly. I had no idea where the journey of racehorse ownership would take us, but that was the very essence of why we did what we did.

The book takes you through our path to ownership, through syndicates and clubs, and ultimately to the sales at Newmarket. It then follows twelve months that we could never have dreamed of, with so many highs and quite a few lows too.

It will hopefully give prospective owners some idea of what to expect. Racehorse ownership is not something that should be undertaken lightly, but it is also not something to be feared.

The industry is a friendly one, and if you have a query, a quick telephone call or email will generally give you the answer that you are looking for. I find the customer service at Weatherbys Bank so much better than my mainstream banking providers.

Social media can also be very supportive, but be warned, it can also be a toxic place too.

There are many benefits to being a racehorse owner, but outside of the obvious of watching your horse run, I have barely scratched the surface of these.

However, I do feel that we have made the most of the different relationships that we have struck up, and as a result, we have made many new friends.

I have to give particular thanks to my wife, Sally, for sacrificing much of her own riding experience to accompany me to the races. Of course, that has also meant that she has had to shop far more than she would like for an endless stream of new outfits. It just would not do to be seen on television wearing the same hat or fascinator at Newbury in August that was also worn at Redcar in April.

Luke Lillingston and his wife, Tabitha, have been a constant throughout the year, with Luke always being the first one on the post-race telephone call. His eye for a racehorse goes without saying, but he is always there with advice, guidance and connections whenever they have been required.

I will always be grateful to Simon Chappell for making the introduction to Luke, but also for his input and suggestions before we had decided on a purchase, as well as throughout the summer.

Richard Kent has been a great friend with some sound advice, and he has been as interested in the progress of our racehorses as anyone. It was Richard's idea to include a glossary of terms, a suggestion that will hopefully remove some of the mystifying terminology unique to the industry. The glossary is by no means comprehensive, and it focuses on flat racing. For National Hunt racing there will be additional terms, and some of the terms associated with flat racing will have different meanings.

David O'Meara and his team, with Jason, Aaron, Maddy, Gina, Char-lee, Sarah, Gabi, Di and many more have been ultra-professional and always very welcoming whenever we have visited the yard or seen them at the track. Similarly, Tim Easterby has been a friendly face on many occasions, with kind words about Star Of Lady M as well as updates on Emerald Duchess. His team is very much based around a family affair, including his wife, Sarah, and sons, William and Thomas, but there is also Tom, Rory, Geordie,

Nicky and several others who have helped to make our experience so complete. I would highly recommend either of our trainers, but at the same time you need to find one that will give you exactly what you want.

Ed Harper from Whitsbury Manor welcomed us through his gates, and his team were one of the first to thank us at the sales. Understanding the desire for speed at Whitsbury was a great insight.

Finally, our jockeys. Star Of Lady M has been ridden by Danny Tudhope, Jason Watson and Colin Keane, whilst Emerald Duchess has had Duran Fentiman, David Allan, Cam Hardie and Sean Kirrane on board. My thanks to each and every one, as they all strive for success on our behalf.

Our first year of racehorse ownership has given us great pleasure, and reliving every moment in writing this book has also been a wonderful experience.

We have decided that it would only be fair to give something back, and therefore all profits from the book will be donated to the Injured Jockeys Fund and the Retraining Of Racehorses charities.

I hope that you enjoy reading it, and that it will perhaps encourage you to enter the world of racehorse ownership. Racing clubs and syndicates are a great way to start. They are relatively inexpensive, and they will get you close to the action. Many trainers now have their own syndicates, but there are plenty of independents too. I have listed a number of racing clubs and syndicates at the back of the book. Research as many as you can so that you can select the one that is right for you.

If, like us, you are ready to become a fully-fledged owner, I wish you good luck. There is nothing quite like the thrill of seeing your racehorse compete. These magnificent athletes, full of beauty and power, can take you on the most incredible of journeys. See you at the sales.

Chapter One

I was brought up in the 1960s and '70s in Ashton-Upon-Mersey, a small suburb of Sale in Cheshire. Ashton was undoubtedly a town, but the small row of shops that bordered the high street was always referred to as Ashton Village. There were two pubs, a newsagent, launderette, sweet shop, haberdashery, greengrocer, butcher, hairdresser, and various other shops typical of the era.

It was clear just by looking at these emporiums what they offered. The sweet shop had cards and candy in the window, the greengrocer had fresh produce neatly stacked outside, and the newsagent had the latest news headlines on a sandwich board on the pavement in front of it. There were two exceptions to this. The first one was the dentist, whose "house of pain" was through a narrow door at the top of a flight of two steps. The second one was set a few feet back from the main street, with a greyed-out window that completely obscured what was inside. The door was never left open; it automatically swung shut as soon as it was released. The only clue as to the nature of its business was the wording above the window. "TURF ACCOUNTANT" printed in small, drab letters. I had no idea what a Turf Accountant did, and my dad was reluctant to tell me. It was as though the owners did not want to reveal their business, and their customers were happy to maintain the anonymity.

However, in the spring of 1973, I was left waiting on the pavement whilst my dad went inside. He was placing a bet on the Grand National, and so at eleven years old my interest in horseracing began. I tried to peep in through the door, but it closed rather quickly, and what I could see was shrouded in cigarette smoke.

My eldest sister, four years my senior, seemed to know a lot about horses. She was a regular at the local riding school, and she was sweet on the chances of Crisp. I never found out what my dad had backed, but I was always one for the underdog, and at the last fence Red Rum was certainly the underdog. Of course, he came through to win, repeating his triumph twice more, with two seconds in between.

The Grand National was a landmark in the sporting calendar after that, but I also discovered that there was more to the sport than Aintree. Lester Piggott's name featured regularly in the sports pages, and I always looked for his mounts rather than those of his arch rival, Willie Carson. The Derby win of The Minstrel in 1977 was a particular favourite, but at that stage, the horseracing world was just a series of names, numbers and the odd flash of excitement on the television.

Chapter Two

In August 1978, I began working at a local brewery in Stockport. Although I worked in the offices as a trainee in the fledgling computer department, I became friends with several of the blue-collar brewery workers. Horseracing was a popular topic of conversation, and they organised regular trips to the various racetracks within a reasonable drive of the town.

Just down from the brewery there was a bookmaker's shop, which I discovered was a much more common name for the Turf Accountant. I stepped inside, still officially too young to place a bet, and was fascinated by what I saw. There were no televisions. A man stood in a slightly elevated position at the front of the shop. His job was to pin up paper sheets containing the races in sequence, and mark the odds against each horse. His information came over a radio feed, and he would often cover several races simultaneously. The commentary of the races brought the sport to life, but it could be frustrating as the odds for the next race would often interrupt a crucial part of the current one. After a race was over, he marked the winners and placed horses, together with their odds. These had to be made available for the whole day, so that people could come in at any time and check how their horses had done.

The sides of the shop were plastered with the pages of the *Sporting Life* and *Sporting Chronicle*, with slips of paper and tubs of small pencils dotted here and there.

The slips of paper were, of course, betting slips, and the floor would quickly become awash with them. Pencils would be discarded everywhere along the shelves. The final part of the shop was the betting counter. Two windows were to place bets, and one was for the payout. The betting slips were single sheets. You handed them over with your stake, they were photocopied, and handed back. After an hour or so, you realised that the place was getting increasingly smoky as the punters became ever more desperate.

Betting became a habit. I discovered the joys of the Trixie, Yankee, doubles and trebles (long before the creation of the Lucky 15). I also discovered that before the daily horseracing began, there was often greyhound racing too. In the event of bad weather there would be trotting races. The only occasions that you could not have a bet were on Sundays, Good Friday, and Christmas.

My first big winner came in the spring of 1979. The racing press was full of the news that American jockey Steve Cauthen was on his way to England. Cauthen had won the US Triple Crown in 1978, and he was on board Tap On Wood in the 2,000 Guineas at Newmarket. I knew nothing about the horse, but Cauthen seemed fair value at 20/1, and so it proved. He also triumphed in the 1,000 Guineas and Oaks with Oh So Sharp and the Derby with Slip Anchor six years later, and I backed him in all three of those classic wins.

Later that year, the brewery lads invited me on a trip to York races. It was cold, miserable, and I only backed one winner at a very short price. I absolutely loved it. Subsequent trips were to Haydock and Doncaster, but my favourite was our annual excursion to the Chester Cup meeting.

In 1980, it was once again Steve Cauthen who starred on Arapahos, and I did get to see the mighty Sea Pigeon, though he was probably feeling the effects of his Champion Hurdle victory. At the 1982 meeting, I managed to come away with a photo finish image of the first race, and the text of the Stewards Enquiry which has sadly long since faded.

My favourite racehorse from that era was undoubtedly Shergar. Back in 1981, the Epsom Derby was run on Wednesday, and that afternoon I was in work. I made up an excuse to head into town, and I stood outside a television rental shop to watch the race. The bookmakers still had no pictures, only race commentary. There was a small crowd gathered outside the shop, and as the field raced into the home straight, there were a few asking who was in the lead. There really was no doubt as Shergar won by a record-breaking ten lengths.

Two years later, I backed Corbiere to win the Grand National, my first National winner for quite some time, but the Derby was an open affair. As with Steve Cauthen a few years earlier, I went with the jockey, and sure enough Lester Piggott triumphed on Teenoso. I always liked the opportunity to win big for a small stake, and my 5p Yankee that had Corbiere as the final leg produced a return of more than £400 for my 55p stake (plus tax). The Tote Placepot also promised big payouts, and after a few weeks of attempting to land it, I managed to correctly predict six placed horses at Catterick. The return of £638.40 for my 53p stake, which included 3p tax, is the biggest odds I have ever achieved for a single bet.

The Breeders' Cup was inaugurated in 1984, and the late Saturday night time slot was perfect. The highlight for me came in 1990. Lester Piggott teamed up with Vincent O'Brien to win the Breeders' Cup Mile with Royal Academy in a race that will be remembered forever.

Chapter Three

In 1989, I moved on from the brewery to a large catalogue retailer based in the centre of Manchester. Having served my apprenticeship picking up many computer disciplines, I was ready for a new challenge, and I saw it as a stepping stone to freelance contracting. Just around the corner from the office was a William Hill betting shop, and by then my gambling had progressed to football, golf and American football.

In 1993, my career changed again, and I was offered a contract to stay at the retailer. The following year, it was time to look elsewhere, and I received an offer to work at BT Mobile in Leeds. The contract agency was Esprit Systems, and my contacts there were Maura Kelly and Neil Thornton. Neil was to play a major role in my involvement with racehorses several years later.

A few weeks before my BT Mobile contract, I married Sally, and she shared my love of horseracing. She had an air of "To the Manor Born" about her, and when email became popular a few years later, it was somewhat inevitable that her handle involved Lady Madden. Her friends shortened this to Lady M.

For the first few years of our marriage, with mortgage interest rates at 15%, money was tight despite Sally's full-time job and my freelance roles. As the government threatened to turn the screws on taxing freelancers, I took a permanent role back at the retailer, but this time in a management position.

By then, the leasing of racehorses and the creation of racing clubs was becoming a popular route into racehorse ownership. Previously, we had dabbled with the club format of Elite Racing, but with my new-found career stability, I decided to buy Sally a share through Ownaracehorse. This involved a one-off fee that bestowed ownership for a twelve-month period. The horse in question was Farington Lodge, a gelding and three-mile chaser trained by Joss Saville. We went up to see the horse during an Ownaracehorse stable visit, which was an interesting day out. However, our real thrill came on 8th July 2008 when the horse was declared to run at Uttoxeter.

The Staffordshire course is one of the nearest to our home, just over an hour by car, and we arrived in good time to savour the whole experience. Chatting to a friend of mine, an experienced gambler, we decided that as our horse was in the last race, and given that many of the syndicate would be present, we should get a bet on early to get the best price. So, we did, with odds of around 12/1.

Tension mounted as the earlier races rolled along, and by the time of our race, with the odds plummeting to 8/1, we were feeling quite pleased with ourselves. However, our trainer's representative said that the horse would need the run, and they were just looking for him to get round safely. He analysed the race perfectly, even giving us the name of the eventual winner. Sure enough, with a circuit to go Farington Lodge was trailing, and being urged for more effort that was clearly not forthcoming.

He eventually finished eighth of the eleven starters, some fifty-seven and a half lengths behind the winner. It was a disappointing result, but an excellent experience, and one that left us wanting more.

Ownaracehorse were clearly an ambitious group, and the next time their name cropped up was with Tesco Tokens. This is where you collect tokens from shopping at Tesco or by using a Tesco credit card. Eventually, you could have enough to get a discount off your shopping, or you could shop with one of Tesco's partners using the tokens instead of cash. In this case, we exchanged them for a share in Friendship Bay and two shares in Tenjack King. Friendship Bay, a gelding trained by James Evans, ran four times during our ownership, finishing second, fourth and third, before finally getting his head in front at Worcester. Unfortunately, we were unable to attend any of his races.

Tenjack King was a flat horse trained by Joss Saville, and during our ownership he was gelded, finished last at York and Beverley, before finally trailing in ninety-three lengths behind the winner at Southwell. He was tenth of eleven in the Southwell race, which happened to be the only one that we attended. Despite the losses, the ownership experience was still something to aspire to. Our last horse with Ownaracehorse was the sprinter, Namir. We saw him finish fourth of ten at Pontefract, but his favourite track seemed to be Bath where he finished first and second. However, Bath was just a little too far for us to travel to.

Chapter Four

By the end of 2010, we decided to take a break from this form of ownership. We were still attending the races regularly, and I organised an annual trip to York in October for the local cricket club.

I had kept in touch with Maura Kelly and Neil Thornton, and whilst at the retailer, I managed to put some business their way. As a reward, in October 2011 they invited me to the Friday meeting of the October finale at York. I cheekily asked if my wife could come too, as we would both be there on the Saturday as part of our annual cricket club trip. That was agreed, and so we prepared for a Friday of drinking, dining and racing in the Ebor restaurant at York.

We travelled up by train, a long journey made slightly more tolerable by upgrading to first class, but on the Manchester to York service I am not convinced this made much difference at all. We arrived in the city in good time and made our way to the course by taxi.

To be greeted with a glass of champagne on arrival at the racecourse is certainly the way to go. After the day in the Ebor restaurant, Sally more or less refused offers of County Stand tickets, preferring to wait for hospitality or something similar.

During the day, we met several of Neil's business associates, including Chris Powell and Simon Chappell. They had a successful business in IT, though not the disciplines that I had made a career in. However, we did find some common ground when we discovered that we had a mutual interest in gambling on American Football. Subsequently, we would have trips to Wembley to watch the NFL live, as well as NFL marathons in Leeds and London. For these, we would take in back-to-back Thanksgiving Day games before finishing off the night in a casino.

On this particular Friday, one of the guests had a runner, and so we were fortunate enough to go into the parade ring to get a pre-race appraisal from the trainer and jockey. We met Mick and David Easterby, and Sally took a selfie with Mick, a ritual that has become almost an annual event.

In the spring of 2012, we were invited to the Grand National meeting as guests of another recruitment company. We were there on "Liverpool Day", and although we were in a hospitality restaurant, it was nowhere near the quality of York, so we were ecstatic to be invited back to the Knavesmire the following October. Quite by chance, as the Marriott was full, we came across Middlethorpe Hall, a National Trust hotel situated next to the course. It is a fabulous venue with excellent staff and beautiful grounds. It became the only hotel that we looked for when attending the races at York.

Simon Chappell became more deeply involved in the ownership of racehorses. This meant that he was not always available for our York race days, which quickly became the first date to be pencilled on to the calendar each year.

Sometimes we would get to go into the parade ring as "Owners", and at other times we were content to soak up the atmosphere in the restaurant.

Chapter Five

In late summer 2012, I went freelance once again, but this time I was determined to create my own business rather than just accepting contract roles. By late 2013, I was working for a payday lender in Nottingham, as well as flying to Washington DC for an assignment with Freddie Mac. As a result, I had more disposable income than previously, and so I decided that we should consider racehorse ownership again. In late 2015, I came across Ontoawinner. This gave ownership of a racehorse for a one-off fee plus monthly payments to cover training. I opted for a yearling colt by Kheleyf, and we were even given the chance to suggest names. Although our choice of name was not picked, the selection of Elements Legacy was actually quite close to my company name of Legacy IT.

Elements Legacy was trained by Karl Burke, and he was to make his debut in June 2016 at York. This was fabulous news, and we headed off for the day. We collected our owners' badges and took up residence in the wonderful Owners & Trainers bar at the course. I even purchased an Ontoawinner tie, though after wearing it at York that day, I do not think that it has been out of the wardrobe since.

The horse was priced at 20/1, and the race was the Rous Selling Stakes. Although it was a seller, it was a Class 3 event, so they must have seen some promise at home. Karl Burke had another horse in the race, and they were consistent, finishing eighth and ninth out of the eleven runners. Elements Legacy was a total of sixteen and three quarter lengths behind the winner, an inauspicious start to his career. A week later, he finished fourth of six in another seller at Redcar, this time Class 6. In July, he finished third in a Class 6 seller at Leicester, and later that month he finished fourth at Yarmouth, recording his best ever rating of 60. The season ended bizarrely. In August, he ran fifth of six at Kempton, and in September he ran in an auction race at The Curragh in Ireland. Hopelessly outclassed, he finished twenty-eighth of thirty. A month later, he was gelded, and that was effectively the end of our involvement as we decided against renewing our ownership for 2017. He did actually run four more times, finishing last on each occasion.

Of course, the trainer and other connections do not always know whether a horse will run well, win, or come last. However, I drew away from racing clubs. Our experience was interesting, but it was probably not the right time for us. I had done little or no research, and we could not really make the most of the opportunities on offer.

In recent times, the various syndicates and racing clubs have become much more innovative and inclusive for their members. The industry too has recognised the vital role that these organisations play in recruiting new owners, and there have been a number of syndicate days at various racecourses to encourage ownership.

Of course, as I have said, often the connections will not know what is to come from a horse. On one occasion at York, Simon Chappell rang a trainer who had a runner in the first. "Will yours be trying?" Simon asked. The answer came back in the affirmative, and so the whole table, and some from the adjoining tables, invested heavily. The horse ran poorly, finishing well down the field. On another occasion, Simon was not at the races but he did have a runner. "We don't know if she has trained on as a three-year-old," he admitted. "I guess we will see today." We adopted a cautious approach and placed just a small bet on her. She absolutely flew home, much to the delight of our table and those around us.

Sally and I had graduated from the Ebor to the Parade Ring restaurant at York, particularly for the Friday evening Music Showcase event. On the first such occasion, the weather was dreadful. Musical guest Tom Jones cancelled as his helicopter would not fly in the storm, and when we got back to Middlethorpe Hall, the power was out. However, it was a fabulous day, topped off by the waiter at Middlethorpe telling ghost stories in the drawing room by candlelight.

We were at York so often that it made sense to get an annual membership. The members bar at York is a cosy spot overlooking the finishing line, and the price was quite reasonable when done as a couple. However, I found myself travelling more and more, and when Covid struck we decided to let it lapse.

In summer 2018, I had one of my favourite bets, and it won at 100/1. I only put £2 on it, but that is not really the point. The bet was that every team in the 2018 FIFA World Cup would score at least once. It went down to the wire, but when Costa Rica equalised in the fifty-sixth minute of their final match against Switzerland, the money was safe.

Chapter Six

In August 2018, there was a seminal moment, without which I would probably not have dared to venture into the world of full racehorse ownership. Simon Chappell made an introduction to Luke Lillingston and Ted Voute, two very influential players in the bloodstock industry. They had an idea to create an online portal to allow buyers and sellers to trade stallion nominations. Chris Powell had access to a team of developers, and so we met up in Manchester to discuss the details. The world of thoroughbred breeding was a revelation. I knew that there were large sums involved, but the complexity, monopolies, good guys and bad guys could have been the ingredients for a thriller, and probably are.

I was involved with Manchester Metropolitan University, and we got the students to come up with some ideas initially, but it soon became clear that the whole business was much more complex than their traditional three-month deliverable.

We set to work, with myself as the Project Manager and Managing Director of Buyanom.com. Although we did not have many face-to-face meetings, we had regular Skype calls and the project was progressing.

Luke recommended that I read *Horse Trader: Robert Sangster and the Rise and Fall of the Sport of Kings*, so I downloaded it to my Kindle. I was already aware of Robert Sangster from my trips to Chester races, where he seemed to have an unbeatable combination with trainer Barry Hills, but this book introduced me to a whole new world. I read it during a transatlantic flight, and I have since read it again. It is a great story in itself, but it also significantly increased my knowledge of the industry that I had just joined.

A few days before we were due to launch Buyanom.com, I headed down to Newmarket to help with preparations. Hats, pens, jackets, and several other promotional items were sourced, and I met with the lovely Francesca Cumani who was to be our presenter for the evening. Our business was inevitably based at Tattersalls, where the sales ring was a fascinating place. Young horses were housed in stables and led to the parade ring prior to their auction. The patter of the auctioneer was incomprehensible. Fortunately, there was an electronic board that explained how things were progressing. I met one of the leading auctioneers, John O'Kelly, afterwards and I was relieved to discover that away from the ring he spoke quite normally.

The launch itself went well, and we ended the night having dinner in the Jockey Club where we met trainer Charlie Hills. He was enjoying a rare night away from his home and family, but he was happy to talk about all manner of things. These included Battaash, the fastest horse in training at the time, and his boys' love of Tottenham Hotspur.

In the following days, I returned to Newmarket and demonstrated our new website to stud farms including Darley, Cheveley Park and Lanwades. We also held an open session at the National Stud, and I was struck by the palatial surroundings that all of the extremely valuable stallions were housed in.

A month later, I went to our second launch, this time at Goffs in Ireland. I met many of the same people, but there seemed to be a much more relaxed approach to everything. The launch was certainly more low-key, and we had to overcome quite a few technical hitches along the way. I stayed at an Airbnb a short drive from the auction site, where the entrance hall was marked by a huge crucifix. My Catholic mother would have been proud of me.

Chapter Seven

Back at home, I accepted another contract role that took me to Kiev on a regular basis. On one of these trips, I learned that my village of Whaley Bridge was under threat as the dam holding back the Toddbrook Reservoir was in danger of collapse, but that's another story.

As the Kiev contract came to a close, I renewed my acquaintance with an old business associate who was now head of Enterprise Modernisation at Google. That led to a multi-year engagement which peaked in the summer of 2021, when I had twenty-five contractors working on a Brazilian assignment. My company had gone from generating turnover of £150,000 annually, to somewhere between £3 million and £4 million. My bank balance grew, as did my leisure time. There was only one thing for it, Sally and I wanted to buy a racehorse. This time, it would not be through a club or a syndicate, this time it would be the whole thing.

When I announced this to my circle of friends, there was great interest. Several of them wanted a piece of it. We had discussed this previously, and I had told them that they needed to come up with between £5,000 and £10,000 each to get it off the ground, which in truth, was never likely to happen.

I figured that with a purchase price limit of £20,000 and a training budget of £30,000, I would need £50,000 to get through the first year. Of course, there were no guarantees, and a vet bill could easily break my budget.

Having decided on the likely costs, my next call was to Simon Chappell. He explained that the options were either one of the sales, or we could get lucky with a private sale. The riskiest purchase would be a foal, and we were not really interested in waiting that long before our purchase saw the racetrack. The yearling sales were also a risky option, but bargains could be had. Our next consideration ought to be the Breeze-Ups, where horses are timed over two furlongs. However, this can have its downside as often the lots are honed for that specific task, rather than the cut and thrust of five furlongs. Finally, there was the horses in training sale where generally we could pick up something that has at least proven itself on the course. Simon also recommended a Weatherbys bank account and membership of the Racehorse Owners Association (ROA).

If anyone knew more than Simon, it was our mutual friend, Luke Lillingston. His proven ability at the sales would be a major asset, and he would understand exactly what we wanted. I also considered Ted Voute, but as his circle included the role of racing manager to Prince Faisal, I thought he might be a bit above our league, in the nicest possible way. So, I spoke to Luke and he immediately took us in the direction of the Book 3 yearling sale at Tattersalls.

The Tattersalls October Yearling Sale is split into four "Books". Each horse to go through the sales ring is rated by the auctioneers, and they are assigned a lot number based on the assessment. These lots are then assigned in ascending order across the four Books. Book 3 ought to have contained a reasonable number of yearlings that would fit into our budget.

Luke suggested that we should choose ourselves a trainer, and that we might also consider finding a local equestrian centre that would break the horse in for us. This would enable us to visit more often than if our trainer was, for instance, in North Yorkshire. He arranged an introduction to David O'Meara, a successful trainer based a few miles outside of York. This seemed ideal, and when we were again heading for the Friday evening Music Showcase meeting at York, with entertainment provided by Rick Astley afterwards, we decided to call at the training yard on the way. From the moment we drove through the entrance and down the sweeping driveways, we could tell that it was a serious establishment. It was like driving into an American ranch, with paddocks, rails, and a few horses dotted here and there. We pulled up in the visitors' car park, and we were greeted by a Jack Russell. The dog bounded straight into the car, somehow found a stray ping pong ball under the seat, and then ran off with it.

I chased after the dog, tempting it with sticks, fearing that if the dog choked on the ball, it would not be the best of starts to our relationship with the trainer. All was well when I outwitted the small canine, and David came to greet us with one of his assistants, Gina. David was off to the races at Thirsk, so he left Gina to show us around and we were immediately impressed. We would be more than happy to send a yearling into David's care, and our decision was made more or less on the spot.

The question of breaking was also not a difficult one. As Sally rides her own horse she knows a few horsey people, and it was soon evident that none of them would be confident about breaking and educating a yearling racehorse. So, we agreed that our yearling would go straight from the sales to David O'Meara's yard.

I rang Tattersalls and asked for a copy of the Book 3 catalogue as soon as it was available, which would be in early August. I also researched the bonus system, and this led us to the conclusion that a filly was a much more sensible purchase than a colt. If we were fortunate enough to win just one race, we could expect a Great British Bonus (GBB) of up to £20,000, and although this was divided between the owner, breeder, jockey, stable and trainer, we would get up to

£13,000 on top of any prize money. Of course, there was no guarantee, but it was a significant factor in our decision.

I registered with Weatherbys and the ROA, paying the first of what seemed like endless registration fees, though with no horse as yet, these were minor tasks. One thing that we could proceed with was the registration of colours. There is a handy tool on the British Horseracing Authority (BHA) website that allows you to experiment with colours and patterns. Many of the combinations are already reserved, but we settled on the rather striking emerald green shirt with black star, emerald green sleeves with black stars, and emerald green cap with black star. I registered them in my name, after paying the relevant fee, and all that we needed then was a horse.

The Book 3 catalogue duly arrived, and I pored over every detail. In truth, I could not hope to dissect the nuances of every pedigree, but by reducing it down to statistics, I thought that I could make a semi-educated shortlist. It did not quite turn out that way. I could easily dismiss anything that was not a filly, and indeed anything that was not a GBB registered filly. A winning dam and siblings were also a consideration, and eventually I narrowed it down to about thirty yearlings.

I met Luke as part of the Turf Club at York's Ebor meeting, and we had a great time as he shared his insight into various aspects of the racehorse. He admitted that he had not yet looked at the Book 3 catalogue, so I was well ahead of him on that one.

Somewhere along the line my research went astray, as when I spoke to Luke on the eve of the sale, he passively rejected all but a couple of my selections. What I mean is that he did not out and out dismiss them, he simply did not include them in his shortlist, which was guaranteed to be far more accurate and relevant than mine.

Chapter Eight

So, we headed to Newmarket on the first day of the two-day Book 3 sale. Traffic was light, and we arrived around 9.30am, in good time for the first lot at 10am. Luke had already been hard at work, which was understandable as he also had horses to sell at the sale. Our first choice was Lot 1330, a Havana Grey filly. The sale began at Lot 1311, so she was twentieth into the ring, and at the rate of twenty-six lots per hour she was due to go under the hammer within the first sixty minutes. We left the parade ring area and climbed a few steps to take our seats in the sales arena, nursing our £20,000 budget. Of course, sales are quoted in guineas, and we were not going to lose out for that extra 5%. Nerves were fairly calm at this early stage of proceedings.

The bids opened, and in a flash our budget was left far behind. She eventually went for 82,000 guineas, and if that was a sign of things to come, we would struggle to find something within budget. On the positive side, if we had bought our first selection, we would have missed out on two exciting but exhausting days.

Luke knew almost everyone at the sale, and he introduced us to Jason Kelly. Jason is the racing manager for David O'Meara, and so when we did eventually make a purchase, he would be partly responsible for her care.

Luke led us on a trail of stables, pulling out horses at each one, inspecting them, slapping them, measuring them, and watching them walk. Each one seemed to have a different thing that would lead to them being crossed off, but one or two did make the shortlist. However, prices in the ring were still high, and none of those that we had earmarked so far looked like falling within our budget.

Sally and I quickly checked into our hotel, and then we returned to excellent burgers for lunch. Suitably refreshed, we resumed our journey around stables and yards. We did not have many in the sales ring, and most of the research was put towards the next day's lots. At around 5pm we crossed over to Luke's flat, where his wife, Tabitha, was preparing a lovely meal. We had one more filly, by Havana Gold, to bid on that day, but she was in the last few lots so we had time to spare.

As the sale progressed, we returned to the ring, where our Havana Gold filly was due to appear. The bidding started much more slowly, and for the first time we were actually able to enter the contest. 18,000, 20,000, and at 25,000 Luke asked if we wanted to continue. I decided against it, and the filly eventually went for 28,000 guineas, almost 50% above our budget. This was more encouraging and gave us hope that we might make a purchase the following day. Luke and Tabitha were excellent hosts, probably too good in fact, as the red wine flowed. We got a taxi to our hotel, and we were a little bleary eyed for our early start the next morning.

Chapter Nine

Luke had a Covid related family crisis, but he was already hard at it when we arrived at Tattersalls. As the sales began again, it was clear that the prices were still running rather high, but that just meant looking at even more horses to find the right one.

We visited almost every stud in the place, too numerous to mention, though three stood out. At Mickley Stud, Richard Kent was singing the praises of the offspring of his stallion, Massaat. Luke was impressed, so much so that he shortlisted two of them. Richard and I have a mutual friend that he knows as a racehorse breeder and I know as a cricketer. We talked about horses, cricket, and drinking in the Peak District village of Disley. He said that if we ever considered creating a syndicate, we should go straight back to him. At Whitsbury Manor, we shortlisted a Havana Grey filly, but we looked at several others. One of these somehow got loose and raced across the grass towards where we were standing. At the last second, I sidestepped the runaway horse, and there was no harm done. It could easily have been very different. I could have been knocked out cold, and woken up to the news that we had purchased who knows what.

At Minster Stud, Willie Carson was the proud owner. We looked at some of his, but none made the final list. However, Willie had lost none of his old charm, and we spent a wonderful fifteen minutes or so chatting about horses.

We had a list of about ten, and we were ready to do battle. First, though, it was time for lunch. Ted Voute joined us and we discussed the high prices. He was off for a dinner with Prince Charles that evening, and Sally jokingly commented that he was having quite a day, the Maddens for lunch and Prince Charles for dinner.

It was time for second inspections, and this reduced the shortlist further. One of the remaining fillies came to the parade ring and did not please Luke's eye, so that was another one gone. We added a Cityscape filly, as although Cityscape was considered unfashionable, there could be some value to be had there. With time running out, we were left with just four options, one by Havana Grey, one by Cityscape, and two by Massaat. However, we were quite prepared to leave with nothing and live to fight another day. Our purchase had to be right for us.

The Havana Greys were commanding big prices, as were the Massaats, though I did think that the Cityscape filly would fall well within our budget.

Everything else was struck off our list, and so there was the very real possibility that we would leave the sales empty-handed. Having spent the best part of two days in search of our filly, I was just a little nervous. It was late on the second day, and we headed for the sales ring.

The Havana Grey filly was first up, and as she was paraded there were a few colts acting up. She took it all in and remained calm, which was a good sign. As she was about to enter the sales ring, we took up our seats, and I noticed that the auctioneer was John O'Kelly.

Part of his job is to get the best possible price, and he does this by offering as much information as possible, giving buyers time to make up their minds. As a buyer, you want him to bring the hammer down as quickly as possible. Bidding commenced, and it was a reasonably slow start. Two thousand, three, four, five, seven, eight, ten. We went to twelve. Thirteen was bid against us. Luke looked at me for approval and I nodded. We went to fifteen. The other bidder dropped out. John O'Kelly scoured the room for more clients. His patter became unbearable as we were on the brink of securing our purchase. His eyes went left and right. His spotters looked up and down. He began to draw the lot to a close in an agonisingly slow dance. Finally, a short, sharp tap with his hammer and the filly was ours. 15,000 guineas, a full 5,000 under our budget. A wave of emotion was quickly replaced by delight. We were thrilled and apprehensive at the same time. We were about to embark on a journey that promised to be exciting, but which we knew very little about.

Chapter Ten

Luke was first to offer his congratulations, followed by a Tattersalls representative who provided us with a ticket to demonstrate our purchase. The under bidder was renowned ex-jockey and now racehorse trainer, Jamie Osborne, which gave us more encouragement. The team from Whitsbury Manor came over to offer congratulations and to thank us for our purchase, but there was still much to do. First up, it was a visit to the horse in her stall. She was brought out and we took some pictures. Since she was officially ours, we could study her more closely. She was a beautiful animal, with a very pale grey coat inherited from her sire, Havana Grey. Unlike her sire, her immature mane was black, as was her tail. Her face was marked with the white blaze that had also been passed down from her sire, a trait that could be traced all the way back to her great-great-great-great-grandfather, Northern Dancer and beyond. Now, though, it was on to the more serious business.

With a quick phone call, Luke arranged for her to be insured. The next stage was a wind test, where one of the vets got her to run around in an enclosed arena, travelling in both directions, whilst he listened for abnormalities in her breathing. She was fine, and so we informed Jason Kelly of our purchase. He could expect to receive her at the yard the following day. Transport had to be arranged, and so we went through the Tattersalls offices and organised her collection and delivery. Luke led us through the process like the old hand that he is. Without him, we could have been left to take the horse home in the back of a van.

With the formalities complete, it was time to celebrate. We went back to the bar where Guinness and Prosecco were the order of the day. The television in the corner of the bar continued to show the sale, and we saw that the first of our Massaat fillies went for 35,000 guineas. The Cityscape went for 22,000. Both were beyond our budget, but I guess we might have been tempted up to 25 for the Cityscape filly. The second Massaat filly came into the ring, and Luke dashed off to watch the auction. He wanted to see just who else was interested in Massaat as a stallion.

A few minutes later, he came back into the bar, and I noticed that I had a few missed calls from him. He had actually placed a bid on the Massaat filly which was ultimately unsuccessful. However, she had been sold for just 20,000 guineas. She had been bought by trainer Tim Easterby, and although it seemed a little complicated, it appeared that the breeder Richard Kent wanted to retain a portion of her too. So, we could buy perhaps 75% for 15,000 guineas, and we could then syndicate that out to anyone who was interested. Luke said that we could have the weekend to think about it, so from having no racehorses an hour before, we then potentially had one and three quarters.

The journey home was done in a bit of a dream, but everyone was excited by our purchase. The syndicate took off quickly, with myself and Sally, my sister Fiona and her son Jake (though he was not to know until his birthday the following March), and friend Neil Woolley and his wife, Michelle, agreeing straight away. We had six confirmed, so I let Luke know that the deal could be done, even though we were ultimately looking for ten shareholders.

Neil Thornton provided a seventh member, and with so many promises we thought we might be oversubscribed in our aim to sell ten shares. That did not prove to be the case. As so often happens, enthusiasm is very high until people are asked to put their hand in their pocket, so we ended up stuck on seven. I decided that I could stand the cost of the other three, so although we tried to get rid of those shares, it was not really a showstopper.

The following morning, I rang Richard Kent about the Massaat filly. He was full of optimism, suggesting that she would make her debut at York and then we would go to Royal Ascot. He said she was always the best filly at the farm, and he invited us down to have a look around. I asked him about naming the horse, and he said he would leave that to the ladies, as they enjoy that sort of thing.

There was a lot of admin to get through, including registering the horses' names, transferring the ownerships into my account, and actually paying for our purchases, but I found that the Weatherbys' systems made this relatively easy.

The dam of the Havana Grey filly was named Abraj Dubai. After a quick Google search I discovered that Abraj means "constellation" in Arabic, so "Star" seemed like an appropriate start. However, many of Sally's friends thought that Lady M should also be included. After mulling over several possibilities, we settled on Star Of Lady M, and I duly applied for registration. This was processed quite quickly, and it was rewarding to see Star Of Lady M appear under "My Ownerships" on the BHA racing administration website.

Naming the Massaat filly was a little more problematic, with many more voices involved. Massaat is not easy to translate, but her dam was Caledonia Duchess which gave us some scope. Derbyshire Duchess was suggested, but it seemed that the original Derbyshire Duchess was a whore in days gone by. Ruby Duchess was the next suggestion, but we agreed on Emerald Duchess, given that she would be racing in our emerald green colours.

We also had to come up with a name for the syndicate, and in the absence of any sensible suggestions, I registered The 1891 Group, given that 1891 was the lot number under which Emerald Duchess was sold.

The horse was registered under the ownership of The 1891 Group and partners, with the partners being Tim Easterby and Richard Kent. As Tim was one of the owners, there was never a question of which trainer to use, and she was sent to settle in at Habton Grange in Malton.

I was now a member of the ROA, I had a Weatherbys bank account, and I was registered with the BHA with access to my racing administration page. What I found confusing was that all of these entities are somehow connected. If you ring the BHA, you use a Weatherbys phone number. When you have a Weatherbys bank account, your racing administration invoices magically appear within that account. It is actually very efficient and seamless; I am just not sure why they need so many elements to it.

Regardless, I then had to create an Authority to Act, which basically allows a trainer to make decisions and manage entries on my behalf. So, I did one for David O'Meara and one for Tim Easterby. Next up, it was back to the colours. I ordered a second set, to be delivered to Tim, and whilst I was on the phone to Allertons, I ordered Sally a silk scarf in our racing colours to be put away for Christmas. Of course, a horse cannot just race in anyone's colours. So, I had to "share" my colours first of all with the syndicate, to allow the syndicate to use them, and then with The 1891 Group and partners to allow The 1891 Group and partners to use them. All of these transactions incur a fee which helps to keep the wolf from the Weatherbys door.

The Weatherbys bank account charges a £5 monthly admin fee, but of course, you cannot use that account for the syndicate. I had to create a second account for The 1891 Group, and syndicate accounts incur monthly charges of £15.

Next on the list, it was sponsorship. I had already arranged for Allertons to create Legacy IT Consultants Limited velcro patches for the collar of our silks, but I had to get the sponsorship officially approved. This allows the company logo to be displayed in every race for a nominal fee, in this case £1000 per horse, and to register for VAT.

VAT was a challenge. HMRC have agreed that an owner's racing expenses can be reclaimed for VAT purposes. So, I registered in my own name, and then I registered for the syndicate, including names, addresses, and even National Insurance numbers for all concerned. The registrations took a while to come through, and while I was waiting, I diligently saved all of the racing related invoices.

In the meantime, there was a fee to register for VAT. There was also a fee to register to use the Weatherbys VAT service. Finally, there was a quarterly fee for each VAT return processed. It seemed like a lot of fees to chip away at the budget, but when we got our first VAT refund of more than £4,000 for Star Of Lady M, it made it all seem worthwhile.

Chapter Eleven

By November, the fillies had settled in at their respective yards. They had been broken in and were getting used to their new routine. We decided to pay them a visit, and all was arranged for a Saturday morning. However, the weather was against us. The snow descended, and roads were closed. The route from the Peak District to North Yorkshire would be scary and so we decided to postpone. It was disappointing, but both David O'Meara and Tim Easterby called me afterwards. It was just as bad with them, and it was a wise move to stay put.

A month later, we tried again, this time with more success. Sally, Fiona and myself booked into an Airbnb in Malton, and we dined at the homely Blue Ball Inn. The locals were entertained by an electronic fish that sang a Christmas song when it was activated. I am sure they were very popular in the early 1990s, but it added to the festive atmosphere. Back at the Airbnb, a place that looked like the owners had walked out of the door just as we were arriving, we watched Dream Horse, the documentary about Dream Alliance. Of course, it was inevitable that we should start wondering what the future held for our dream horses.

The following morning, after a leisurely breakfast in the food capital of Yorkshire, we headed to Tim Easterby's yard. Tim had unfortunately contracted Covid, and so we were greeted by his legendary father, Peter Easterby, and his son, William. We also met Tom Denham who runs all of Tim's social media, and he was a great source for pictures and videos from the stable. They showed us around the yard and took us out onto the gallops. Unfortunately, Emerald Duchess was a little too "fresh" to be ridden out, so we had to be content with watching her walk in a custom-made arena. She stood still for pictures and videos, and she was certainly aware of her surroundings and the people around her.

We said our goodbyes and headed to David O'Meara's Willow Farm. Senior head lad Aaron Bateman showed us around, and we went out onto the frosty gallops to watch Star Of Lady M go through her paces. She cantered in line, and that was about all that was expected of her. Back at her stable, she stood patiently for some photos and some fussing from the girls. Both stables were happy with their charges, so we set off for home with nothing more to think about until early spring.

We received regular updates from both yards, with videos of Emerald Duchess out on the gallops, whilst Star Of Lady M was now going upsides other horses. It was clear that she was the more forward of the two, as her parentage suggested that she would be.

In early January, the thought of racing came into sharp focus. We had an email from Habton Grange suggesting that we enter Emerald Duchess into the Tattersalls auction race at Newmarket in October. There were several entry stages, and the first payment was due. Both Tim and Richard Kent thought this a good idea and so she was entered. A short time later, Jason Kelly asked the same question regarding Star Of Lady M, and so of course I agreed. The auction race is restricted to certain Newmarket sales, and there are allowances based on the band the horse appears in. The bands are separated based on purchase price, and we were pleased that Star Of Lady M was in the lowest band (D). Emerald Duchess, having cost 5,000 guineas more, was in band C. The £150,000 prize fund for the race was certainly a good incentive.

In February, I entered the Big Racing Raffle 2022, and I was delighted to win a prize. This was a one-year membership of Nikki

Evans' racing club. Nikki trains in Abergavenny, so there was not much prospect of a stable visit, but the horse in question was an interesting one. Fittleton Ferry is a Class 6 sprinter, previously trained by Brian Meehan. The horse ran over various distances, but really, according to her previous owner, she wants five furlongs. Therefore, there was some confidence that she could turn her poor form around. Rated at 46, she would carry some light weights in handicaps, and she had been to see a specialist to deal with her sore back that had gone undetected throughout her early racing career.

With the worst of the winter behind us, another early closing race appeared on the calendar. This was the Super Sprint at Newbury, and it was not quite as restricted as the Tattersalls race. Tim Easterby and Richard Kent both thought that Emerald Duchess should be entered, and so we paid the first fee. Jason Kelly thought that it was easy to get carried away with early closing races, and he advised against it. We took his advice and left Star Of Lady M out of the race.

Chapter Twelve

It was time to visit our two-year-olds again, and so we arranged a second trip for early March. Neil and Michelle Woolley accompanied us this time, and we stayed at the Mount Hotel, a favourite haunt of racing enthusiasts. Unfortunately, Emerald Duchess had sore shins and so once again, we were unable to see her gallop, but we saw her on the walker and received very positive feedback from everyone involved. We finally got to meet Tim Easterby, and he was quietly pleased with her progress. Sore shins are an occupational hazard for racehorses, particularly young ones, and everyone assured us that it was nothing to worry about.

Over at Willow Farm, Star Of Lady M galloped over a furlong or so. She passed another horse as part of her training, and stable jockey, Danny Tudhope, got off her and told us that she was sharp with good speed. As she was being washed down, he reiterated that she was a speedy filly, which is exactly what she was bred to be.

We were very impressed with both of our trainers, as they each had encyclopaedic knowledge of all of their horses, and they recognised every one, just by sight. Tim showed us a horse that he expected to win at Hexham at the same time as the Cheltenham Festival (it came second), and he presented several other horses, commenting on which track each of them preferred to race at.

Encouraged by our visits, we had thoughts of the season ahead. We were due to go on holiday from 6th April for a week, and so I alerted Jason Kelly in the hope that he could avoid any races during that week. This was just a precaution as we did not expect Star Of Lady M to see a racecourse before May, and with Emerald Duchess having sore shins it was likely to be even later for her.

We decided to pay a visit to Mickley Stud at the invitation of Richard Kent. It was fascinating to see the mares and foals bouncing around the place, in contrast to Massaat who was happy just to lie down in his stable. This all changed when he had a walk-in cover to attend to, and we were somewhat taken aback when it all happened in front of us as we stood by the covering shed. Sally videoed it, though this may have been in dubious taste. It was all over in around a minute, and Massaat returned to his stable looking pleased with himself, and no doubt ready for another nap. Over a pleasant lunch, Richard informed us that he and his connections were quite keen on Evolicatt in the Brocklesby two days away.

Chapter Thirteen

The flat season starts at Doncaster in March. The traditional opener is the Brocklesby, a two-year-old race that is always keenly anticipated. Evolicatt, a filly by Massaat, was declared as Richard had said. There was a second Massaat runner, a colt named Mascapone, as well as Rocking Ends, a Havana Grey gelding. We were keen to see these run well, as it would perhaps indicate the potency of Massaat and Havana Grey who were both first season sires, which meant that this was their first crop of runners. Evolicatt opened at 12/1, drifted to an incredible 80/1, then plummeted to 15/2. With two-year-old races it is clear that no one really knows very much at all until they have actually raced. The Brocklesby was competitive for much of the way, but when Persian Force flew clear, it was an impressive performance. Evolicatt came in fifth, one place behind Mascapone. Rocking Ends was well beaten. Persian Force cost 225,000 euros as a yearling, quite a way over our budget.

Meanwhile, Jason called back and said that Star Of Lady M had been up to Malton to run on grass. She had done well, and they would be taking her again the following week. If she came out of that with no issues, she would be ready to race. The target was a contest at Redcar on Monday 4th April, two days before we were due to go away. This was a bit of a shock, and something that we were not quite ready for. Jason sent us another video, clearly showing Star Of Lady M running past other horses on the Malton grass, and he said that Redcar was on.

It had been a few years since Sally retired from her role in the NHS, but during the pandemic she volunteered her time at Stepping Hill Hospital, twenty minutes from where we live. She took every precaution, scrubbing herself in the garage before rejoining the family, but on Monday morning, two days after the Brocklesby, she tested positive for Covid. She had been in her voluntary role for around two years, but now, just as the flat racing season was getting under way, she succumbed to the virus. She had seven days to produce a negative test. It would have been a devastating blow to get this far, and then to miss Star Of Lady M's first race.

At the entry stage, six days before the Redcar race, there were quite a few entries. Four had run the previous Wednesday, and four had run in the Brocklesby, including the runner-up. Richard Hannon had trained the winner of the Brocklesby, and he had two entered. Trying to second guess who would actually line up was a fruitless exercise. Would the previous runners find this race too soon? Would Hannon's be as good as his previous winner? This was only the fourth two-year-old race of the season and there was very little to go on.

Tuesday, Wednesday, Thursday and Friday all produced positive Covid test results for Sally who was now self-isolating.

The declarations were confirmed on Saturday 2nd April, and that was the moment that it really sank in. We were actually going racing with our very own horse. Sally was still testing positive for Covid, but we had everything crossed that she would be clear of it in time.

The bookies had Star Of Lady M at 8/1, and she was up against seven other horses. One of these, Primrose Ridge, had finished second in the Brocklesby, and she was the odds-on favourite. Zephina had finished fifth at Kempton five days earlier. The rest were all newcomers. Kevin Ryan, who often excels with his juveniles, had an expensive runner, whilst Tim Easterby had two in the race. Comments on Star Of Lady M ranged from "interesting newcomer" to "judged on breeding others are more appealing". This was a restricted race, which meant that we got a 2lb allowance from all band C horses, and it was Class 5 which is the lowest grade that still qualifies for the GBB.

Chapter Fourteen

On Sunday morning, we received the wonderful news that Sally had tested negative. She did a second test just to be certain, and it confirmed that she was once again fit and well.

Excitement grew as race day approached. The odds swung wildly. I decided to back Star Of Lady M each way at 17/2 the night before, but by the next morning she was out to 12/1. Any local bookies must have taken a fortune as the whole of the village bet on her, as did most of my family.

Redcar is quite a distance from Whaley Bridge, so we set off at 8.30am hoping to get there for when the gates opened at 11. Jason Kelly called on the way up. He explained that we would try to tuck in behind the two horses with experience, and then see how it went. Regardless of the outcome, our jockey, Danny Tudhope, would give her an education on her first start. He did feel that inexperience could be her downfall, but we were hopeful of a good showing.

We drove towards the town and followed the signs that took us through a graveyard to get to the course. Hopefully that was not a bad omen. We were actually ten minutes early arriving, and it is fair to say that Redcar were not quite ready for us. We were given a very friendly welcome, and we were asked to bear with them. It was their first meeting of the new season, and no one could quite remember what to do, but on the stroke of 11am we stepped inside. We were certainly first there, and we strolled past the smart Winners' enclosure and the parade ring. It was blissfully quiet, but we could picture how that would change in a few short hours. Our arrival at the Owners & Trainers facility was clearly too soon, as it was still being cleaned. We got coffees, and settled in for a long wait. We could have had the complimentary lunch, but nerves were on edge and we decided to wait.

I remember frequently waiting to bat for my local and very amateur cricket club, when I had to move away from the rest of the team to tackle my nerves. This was a different level altogether. It was difficult to concentrate, and I just wanted to get on with the action. I was thankful that at least we were in the first race of the day.

The printed racecard proudly bore the name Star Of Lady M, with owner M Madden and displaying our new colours. The Tote boards were showing us at odds ranging from 4/1 to 20/1. The bookmakers had us at a reasonable 7/1, as Primrose Ridge shortened from 6/5 to 1/2 and then 2/5. As the race drew closer, we shortened to 9/2.

We headed downstairs to the bar. Sally wanted port or sherry, but that was a bit of a stretch for Redcar. I had a pint and sipped it, constantly monitoring the time. Our nervousness increased as the clock ticked around, but we met Tim Easterby and Tom Denham in the bar. They kept us occupied and took our minds off the race. There was the welcome view that the two that Tim had running against us were not expected to feature at the business end of the race.

Finally, it was time to go. We went to the parade ring where we met Char-lee Heard from the yard. I asked her what would happen if we didn't finish in the first three. Did we just go home, or would we see our horse afterwards? She said we could go back to the parade ring where the horse would be unsaddled. Danny came out looking resplendent in our emerald green and black starred colours. He reiterated what Jason Kelly had said in that he hoped to cover her up behind the two horses that had raced previously.

Jason Watson, the second jockey associated with David O'Meara's stable, was on the favourite. I asked Danny if he had spoken to Jason about how good the favourite was. He had not, but interestingly enough, Jason had asked him about our filly. Confidence grew, but only a little. Danny was calm, we were not. As she headed for the start, we took up a position on the steps overlooking the finishing line.

I had never considered owning a National Hunt horse, I am not sure my nerves could stand it. It was bad enough worrying about a straight five furlongs. With a jumper, I would be in turmoil over every obstacle. At the start the horses milled around. Fingernails were shredded. Star Of Lady M went into the stalls with no problem, so step one was complete. The starter raised his flag and they were off. She broke well enough, so we crossed off step two. However, the plan was abandoned when Primrose Ridge and Zephina went to our left. We were exposed, but up with the pace. The favourite led, but around two furlongs out, Jason Watson was hard at work. Danny moved Star Of Lady M up to challenge. He was going well. The expensive Insolente switched to the inside and looked a threat along the rail. Danny went in front. A head, a neck, half a length.

The angle was poor and it looked as though Insolente was gaining, but he was actually a length back. Primrose Ridge was beaten, Insolente was held. Zephina finished quickly but well behind. With 100 yards to go we had it sewn up. We both shouted, "Go on, Star", and then looked at each other in astonishment. We were close to tears. Our baby girl, purchased for just 15,000 guineas back in October, had won her first race. The feeling was even better than scoring my first hundred at cricket. Even better than the experience of when Ole Gunnar Solskjaer scored the winner in the 1999 Champions League final, as I watched on from the stands at the Nou

Camp. The winning prize was about £4,000, but she had also claimed a GBB of £20,000, of which we earned 65%. The yard, jockey, trainer and breeder also benefitted from this windfall.

As we left the grandstand, it must have been obvious that we were the winning connections as everyone wanted to congratulate us.

We headed back to the parade ring where Tim Easterby commented that we had a nice filly. He also pointed out that we were in the wrong place. We should have been in the Winners' enclosure. We were still in a dream. Char-lee collected us and led us to the place reserved for the winner, where Danny had just dismounted. It was clear that he loved the horse, giving her reassurance before and after the race. It was also clear that she responded to him. The next twenty minutes were a bit of a blur. Sally had already had a selfie with Danny in the parade ring (of course), but now lenses were clicking and microphones appeared from everywhere. The Redcar chaplain presented us with a memento of the race, a pot bearing the logo and a picture of Redcar racecourse, and we smiled for more photographs. We gave our details, and then we were invited inside for a review of the race and a glass of champagne.

The Redcar technicians were struggling to get the television working, but we took our time to savour the champagne. Sally sat in the huge throne made available to winning connections, and then the race appeared on the screen. We watched it several times, with more champagne, and Redcar prepared a USB copy of the race for us. We thanked our hosts and headed back to the Owners & Trainers bar, as the Redcar staff packaged everything up for us for collection on our way out.

Sally wore her lucky green and black starred scarf, and that morning I had put on my underwear inside out before correcting my mistake. Would these superstitions now have to follow us for every race?

We sat outside, oblivious to the biting wind, and contemplated what had happened. Our phones exploded with messages of congratulations, and then they started ringing. Fittingly, Luke Lillingston was first up. We had originally asked him to buy us a racehorse. Nine days into the season she had already won. Richard Kent, breeder and co-owner of Emerald Duchess, was thrilled for us.

Tweets appeared rather quickly, including one in Arabic. The rest of the day's racing was somewhat irrelevant. We couldn't really get into it. Danny rode a second winner for David O'Meara, and I backed him when he was runner-up on another O'Meara horse, but we decided to head home. We celebrated with a few beers in the Drum & Monkey, our local pub, and looked forward to our next outing.

The calls continued to come in, notably from David O'Meara. He was pleased that we had given him his first winner of the official new flat season, and of course his first two-year-old winner, as it gave the yard a great buzz. Ed Harper of Whitsbury Manor passed on his thanks too, as this was the first winner by first season sire, Havana Grey.

Jason Kelly thought she ran a bit green, and had her entered into a race at Beverley on 21st April. That suited us just fine as it was a week after we returned from holiday, and I suggested that the important date for us was the Marygate at York on Friday 13th May.

In the following days, Star Of Lady M was officially rated as 51 on TopSpeed with a Racing Post Rating (RPR) of 75, so as Simon Chappell pointed out, at that moment in time she was the highest-rated two-year-old filly in the country.

Five days later, another filly came out and topped her rating, but we still have that few days that can never be taken away.

The day after the Redcar race, we received a reassuring message that Star Of Lady M was fine after her exertions, and she was almost ready to race again.

Chapter Fifteen

Twenty-four hours later, we set off for the Dominican Republic. As we waited at Manchester airport, I received another call from Jason Kelly. They were considering running Star Of Lady M at Ripon on 14th April as there was a good chance that the race would cut up to a relatively small field, and she would only have to carry a 4lb penalty as opposed to 7lbs at Beverley. There were only twelve entries and four of them were trained by David O'Meara, so it seemed that Jason's assumption could well be correct. The problem with Ripon was that we would miss the race, as we would be travelling home on that day.

She was also briefly entered at Lingfield on 16th April, but when the dust settled, the conclusion was that Ripon would give us a much better chance. The going at Ripon was described as Heavy, which was not ideal, but it did begin to dry up. By the time declarations were made, forty-eight hours before the Ripon race, two things had happened. Firstly, the going was changed to Soft, which was the same as at Redcar, and secondly, the race was reduced to six runners. Two of them had run in the Brocklesby, finishing sixth and eighth, and as we had already beaten the runner-up, we should have been confident. There were also three unraced horses, and soon afterwards, one of these was listed as a non-runner.

As we were travelling back from holiday and could not be in attendance, two of my nephews represented us at the course. They had an absolutely fabulous day out. Paul took his partner's father, Neil, whilst Jake took his fiancée, Aimee. It was an unbelievable experience, meeting the horse, chatting to the jockey, and enjoying the privileges of the Owners & Trainers area.

Fortunately, if things went to plan, we would be able to catch the race at Paris airport during our lengthy layover. Our flight from the Dominican Republic was delayed, putting the plan in jeopardy, but we somehow made up the time. We landed at Paris and were in the lounge in good time for the race. British bookmakers do not allow live streaming of races outside the UK, and Sky Go is not available in France, so we searched for another feed. I found William Hill TV, and we settled in to count down the forty-five minutes until the race.

Jet lag was quickly dismissed as pre-race nerves once again began to kick in. Jason Kelly called and said we would try to start quickly, but Beach Breeze, eighth in the Brocklesby, was drawn on the rail and would likely lead. The plan was to track him and make our move from half way.

Unlike at Redcar, Star Of Lady M was a hot favourite, as short as 4/7 in places, and the pundits were all over her. She drifted in the betting, eventually going off at 10/11, but we were still confident, and she looked well in the parade ring.

At the post, we had a major concern as Danny Tudhope was off her back and trying to tighten her saddle. Two stall handlers tried to calm her, but she was getting agitated. Fortunately, the situation was resolved, and although she was looking around, she was led calmly into the stalls. Four of us crowded around the laptop, praying that the internet connection did not fail. We had turned off our phones, as there was a slight delay with the laptop feed compared to the live action, and we did not want to get congratulations or indeed commiserations mid-way through the race.

Moments later they were off, and as predicted Beach Breeze took the lead along the rail. The two newcomers were hopelessly outpaced; one of them lost about eight lengths at the start. Teatime Tipple, sixth in the Brocklesby, was under pressure early, and Star Of Lady M raced on the shoulder of the leader. By half way, the leader was under strong driving and we were cruising. Danny let out a little bit of rein and she pressed on, taking the lead and soon going clear. Ole was impressed, but he did not know how far there was still left to race. I was confident as soon as I saw Beach Breeze come under pressure. She was never asked a serious question and won by an easy three and a half lengths, with Teatime Tipple running on for second place. With the naked eye, it looked like four or five lengths, but we were happy to settle for the official distance.

The airport lounge soon knew about it, and once again the phone started ringing. Luke, of course, and then Jason. The Marygate was on everyone's mind. This is a Class 1 Listed race at York in May, a huge step up in class, but she deserved her chance. Her TopSpeed rating was announced as 80, a significant increase from 51, and her RPR was 83, up from 75. She was now rated better than her mother. As an historical benchmark, the first three in the last running of the Marygate were rated 68, 77 and 81 before the race.

Richard Kent was more ambitious, expecting us to get calls from California to get her racing over there. Beverley racecourse tweeted that she looked an ideal horse for their showpiece Hilary Needler race. York racecourse came back and suggested the Marygate was first. Star Of Lady M was in demand.

She had won another decent prize, just short of £4,000, and she had also won another bonus. This was a total of £10,000, reduced as she was in a mixed race that was open to colts and geldings as well as fillies. Again, we received 65%, whilst the rest was distributed to the breeder, jockey, trainer and stable. As for Star herself, she was just fine.

When we got back to Whaley Bridge, it was off to the Drum again for drinks. My nephews returned from Ripon and handed over a nice picture, USB recording of the race, racecard, and another memento, this time a plate. The USB was a permanent fixture in the television, as we showed the race to anyone who was interested, and probably quite a few who were not.

Go Racing In Yorkshire were very pleased as she had now won at two different Yorkshire tracks. This set her firmly in their sights as the "Yorkshire Wonder Horse", a £100,000 prize for the first horse to win at all nine Yorkshire courses before the end of 2023. I thought this was a particularly difficult task, and many good judges considered it to be an impossibility.

Chapter Sixteen

A brief message from Char-lee at Willow Farm told us that Star Of Lady M was safe and sound. As the next forty-eight hours unfolded, we were happy to confirm that she was almost certainly en route to the Marygate. She had a month or so to recuperate between the Ripon race and the York showpiece. Two days later, I got a call from Ed Harper at Whitsbury Manor, keen to know our plans. To have a multiple winner by Havana Grey was great, but to have a Listed winner, or even placed horse, would be another step up. Ed was delighted that we would head for the Marygate, but a few weeks later it seemed that it would not be a straightforward passage.

Jason called again and informed us that he had entered her into the Two-Year-Old Trophy at Redcar. This is another Listed race with an early closing date. It is run on 1st October, the same day as the Tattersalls October auction race, and according to Jason, it was just to keep her options open. Almost immediately, we got the same notification from Tim Easterby regarding Emerald Duchess.

We had time to breathe after two races in quick succession, and we took advantage of the service provided by the racecourse photographers to get some additional prints.

I have already mentioned that the VAT service proved to be useful as we received a refund in excess of £4,000 for Star Of Lady M, going back to the original purchase. The syndicate took longer to come through, but the VAT refund should have been roughly the same amount. When it did eventually arrive, it was £1,800 short of what was expected. I might not have noticed this, but for the fact that the Star Of Lady M refund had been considerably more. So, I queried it with Weatherbys, and sure enough, they had entered a typo which understated what we should have received. It was quickly put right, and they refunded us one quarter's VAT service charge for the inconvenience.

We decided to visit Tim Easterby again a few days after the Ripon race. There seemed little point in visiting Star Of Lady M as she was now racing regularly. By coincidence, Tim had entered Emerald Duchess into a race at Ripon, so it was clear that she was ready to run. This was a hot topic during the morning at Tim's, but the reality was that he was really looking for a fillies-only race for her, as that would entitle her to a full bonus rather than 50% which would apply to the Ripon race. There were not many of these around, but I did find one at Nottingham the following Tuesday. Tim must have agreed with my suggestion, because the next day she was also entered for that race.

We stayed at the Mount Hotel again, and I noticed that there was a sign on the wall advertising "Teatime Tipple" with a selection of cut-price drinks underneath. We returned from Tim's for breakfast at the hotel, and the owner asked who we had been to visit. We told him about Emerald Duchess, and we also explained that we had another horse at David O'Meara's that had won two out of two. He instantly knew who we were talking about, and told us that his horse came second at Ripon. So, Teatime Tipple was not just an advertising slogan, it was also the name of his racehorse. He was full of praise for Star Of Lady M, and told us that all of the trainers that visit his racing-oriented pub thought she was a smart filly. This was nice to hear, and we looked forward to our next outing.

Emerald Duchess was withdrawn from the Ripon race but declared for Nottingham. As in previous seasons, it looked a hot race, with three of the entries owned by Clipper Logistics. If any of them ran in the Marygate, Danny Tudhope would be claimed to ride.

Of course, the two-year-old season progressed all around us. I was literally counting down the days to the Marygate, twenty-one, twenty, nineteen. Meanwhile, Primrose Ridge came out and won a band D race at Beverley by seven lengths. She easily beat three others from the Redcar race, which surely meant that the form was solid. The pessimist in me said that she must have improved a lot, but others suggested that it just showed how good Star Of Lady M really could be. Insolente, fourth at Redcar, ran poorly, whilst Zephina, one place closer at Redcar, ran a good second to a son of Havana Grey. My mind was in a turmoil, trying to figure out what was a good sign, and trying to ignore everything that might be a bad sign.

The race at Nottingham came around, and Luke gave us an introduction to his second cousin, Richard Pilkington, who is the Chairman of Nottingham racecourse. Richard kindly invited us for lunch in the Directors Box, and so it promised to be an extra special day. Nottingham were very welcoming, and they showed us around as soon as we arrived. Emerald Duchess was in the first race. If we did not know it before, one look at the racecard confirmed that it would be a tough assignment. Geordie, from Tim's yard, said that it was just her first day at school, and Tim certainly likes to treat his two-year-olds with kid gloves. There were thirteen runners, including two that cost 340,000 guineas between them.

I was not as nervous when the Duchess ran, perhaps because it was optimistic to think that she might win, or perhaps because it was a shared responsibility, being a syndicate horse. She started at 125/1, which I thought was a bit too big, but when she missed the break, it was clear that she would struggle. Duran Fentiman, our jockey, pulled her away from the rail where the firm ground was like concrete, and then he had to snatch her up as she passed fading horses. She finished a creditable ninth, beating four of the field. This included the horse that finished tailed off last and which cost 40,000 guineas.

Duran was reasonably pleased with her, explaining his race riding tactics, and passing on the information that she showed a burst of speed in the middle of the race that allowed her to improve. So, after a splendid lunch, we headed for home defeated, but optimistic. I messaged Luke and Richard Kent, who of course, owns 12.5% of Emerald Duchess, and everyone agreed that it was not a terrible result. However, the following day, Tim announced that the firm ground had given her sore shins again and she would need some time to recuperate. A few days later, we got the good news from Tim that she had not actually suffered sore shins and she would continue her training.

She was subsequently scratched from the five-furlong Super Sprint, as Tim thought that she already needed at least six furlongs. Afterwards, she was given a TopSpeed rating of 39, and an RPR of 41. An inauspicious start to her racing career, but one that she must surely improve upon.

Chapter Seventeen

The days to the Marygate continued to tick down, and on days when there was no news, I delved into the statistics of the race. In the last four runnings in May, ignoring the July renewal due to Covid, only two horses had run within fourteen days of the Marygate and finished in the first five. Our idea to rest her after the Ripon race was the perfect tactic.

I then got a phone call from Jason Kelly. He told me that the Marygate looked like being a very hot race, and that we should enter the Lily Agnes at Chester as an option. We could declare in the Lily Agnes and still switch to the Marygate, or even run in both races. The statistics above were still relevant, and even more so when combining both races. No horse had ever won both the Lily Agnes and the Marygate, and only one horse had ever run in the Lily Agnes (finished third) and won the Marygate.

At times like this, you rely on the knowledge of your trainer, but I also trust others around me, particularly Luke. I had a conversation with him, and he let me know that the stud farm had called him and asked why we were going for the Lily Agnes. I played back Jason's message and Luke considered that it was a very professional approach. The Lily Agnes was just nine days before the Marygate, so running in both was an option, but a somewhat extreme one.

I then got an email from James Denley who insured the horse for us. He asked why we opted for the Lily Agnes rather than the Marygate, so I explained the options to him too. Having a runner in the Marygate was the ideal choice for me. It is my favourite course and I would already be there on a hospitality table with Integrity.

However, I also liked Chester, but primarily as a spectator and not necessarily for the good of the horse.

The day arrived for the Lily Agnes declarations. I was on the phone with Jason, and he was ticking down the entries. We were up to seven, but Mark Johnston had still not played his hand, and he had two possibles. Nine would be a large field for the tight turns of Chester, so that would make our mind up. As it turned out, no more declarations came in. There was a field of seven runners, and now it all depended on the draw. Six or seven would probably see us withdraw, but then the news came through. We were drawn two. Almost the perfect berth, and so the decision was made; we would run in the Lily Agnes. If she did well, we would still go for the Marygate.

Zephina was running against us again, but Richard Kent told me that the majority owner was local to Chester which probably explained that. Ocean Cloud had won two out of two for Gay Kelleway, and before the race had been sold to race in America for a quarter of a million pounds. Ocean Cloud's two wins were at Kempton, another sharp track that goes the opposite way to Chester. Absolutelyflawless had won her only start at Southwell, and Dunnington Lad was another previous winner in the field, so it would not be an easy task.

With the ups and downs of the entry at Chester, I completely forgot that Fittleton Ferry was making her debut for her new trainer Nikki Evans at Bath. As it turned out, she finished last at odds of 80/1, but it was still a quietly promising run.

When the declarations became official, Star Of Lady M was installed as the 11/4 favourite for the Lily Agnes, but that price quickly shortened. I had a bet at 7/4, but she continued down to 6/4, 5/4, and even 6/5.

The pundits were all over her. *Sporting Life* considered that with a good draw she should make a bold bid to maintain her 100% record, whilst a prominent racing column suggested that it would be extremely difficult to take on Star Of Lady M.

We decided to rent a car with a driver to take us to Chester, which meant that I could have a small sherry in the morning just to calm my nerves. We arrived early, and once again the course was not open. We got dropped off at the Owners & Trainers car park, but the gate was locked. A helpful chap came along and unlocked it, then we made our way towards the course. Another gate was opened to allow cars onto the course, so we skirted around that, went through another gate, and arrived at the Owners & Trainers restaurant. Apparently, that is not what we should have done. The security staff wondered how we had got that far without having any badges, so they showed us back out across the course to the Owners & Trainers reception area.

The reception area was still not open, so we spoke to a friendly man in dark glasses and a sharp suit. He turned out to be Kevin Keegan, but he was only there as a representative; he would be spending most of the day in a private box.

When we finally got our badges, we were shown to the restaurant where seating had been arranged for lunch. We were on tables grouped by trainer, but as we were the only runner for David O'Meara on the day, we were seated with owners from the stable of Hugo Palmer.

To our left was Charles Ledigo, who admitted that he knew little about horses. He also had a runner in the first, Glorious Angel. He confirmed that, despite the lines in the press, his horse had not been specifically targeted at the Lily Agnes. Charles had a business in Whaley Bridge, and it transpired that he was a business partner of our friend Jane O'Neill. It can be a small world at times. Charles was also the producer for a musical show, and he gave us his email address with an offer to show our budding actor son, Ole, backstage when the show came to Buxton, or somewhere else close to home.

To our right were two real characters. Seamus Burns knew Luke very well, and Luke's father, too. Seamus had bred a Derby winner and an Oaks winner, and he had bred a yearling that was sold for five million guineas at Tattersalls. Seamus got fed up with the waiter service for the bar, and so he decided to serve himself. We shared a few glasses of wine as we talked about horses and his companion Ken Webb. Ken more or less ran the point-to-point races at Tabley, and he invited us to join him at the mid-May meet. Although we could not make the date, Seamus ensured that I had Ken's number should we wish to avail ourselves of the free passes on offer.

Seamus and Ken did not have a runner. Seamus had more or less retired from the hands-on breeding operation, but they seemed to know everyone and made their way out to the parade ring for several races.

I called Jason and there was a subtle change to the stable narrative. Previously, he discussed which horses might cause us a problem, but now it was all about his confidence. The all-weather form should be beatable, we had already beaten Zephina, we had a good draw, and therefore we had a great chance of winning. It had rained quite a bit, and was still raining as we went out to see our filly.

Confidence was even higher as we had won on Soft and Heavy (there seems to be some dispute about exactly what the ground was at Ripon).

Michael Owen came over to chat to us in the pre-parade ring, well actually he came over to chat to Seamus and Ken but we just happened to be with them. He did seem to have an interest in our filly, but more so in the chances of Glorious Angel who was trained by Hugo Palmer at Michael's Manor House stables.

However, all was not well. Star Of Lady M was normally a very laid-back horse, but she was on her toes and anxious. She carried this into the parade ring, and although we tried to banish it from our thoughts, it remained as a nagging doubt.

We met Richard Kent who thought that our filly looked wired, and would perhaps benefit from a month off. She had not raced for three weeks, so that did not quite make sense, but Richard is a good judge in these matters. Despite the agitation, she did win best turned-out horse, a welcome prize collected by our groom.

Our jockey was once again Danny Tudhope, and he was reserved but confident as we talked through the tactics. He ought to be able to lead on the rail, but definitely did not want to get boxed in.

It was time for Danny to get on board, and we were then intercepted by the ITV film crew. Matt Chapman wanted to know all about Star Of Lady M, even more so Lady M herself. He asked me about the going and left us with the parting words of "Licensed to thrill". It was a welcome distraction as the race drew nearer.

We made our way to the viewing area, which was not great. It was on the inside of the course, and as we looked back down the straight, the big screen was angled away from us. Suddenly they were off. Star Of Lady M bolted down the inside, and Danny worked her to maintain a position with the blistering pace. It was clear that the horse was fighting him, and as they came into the home straight, she edged right, which is the worst thing to do on a left-handed track. She battled gamely, but ultimately finished last, four and a half lengths behind Absolutelyflawless. She had nothing left to give, having burnt her energy leaving the starting gate. It was disappointing, but Danny had eased her down over the last 100 yards to avoid any distress.

I was numb. We had never tasted defeat before, and even after just two races, I thought that we were invincible. We were beaten by the better horse on the day, but I was convinced that on another day, at another course, we would have overcome that field. The bookies agreed, sending her off the odds-on favourite at 10/11, and at such a short price, the stable had to give an explanation to the stewards. They gave the statement that "The filly was unsuited by the tight track on this occasion".

Danny was gutted at the result, and the fact that she did not show her true form. He thought she would benefit from a straight track, and from using her speed at the end of a race to pick off the leaders, as she had done at Redcar and Ripon.

Richard and Seamus both confirmed their thoughts that she should have a month off. I thought that if she was wired then maybe she needed to run again. Luke sided with this principle more than the idea of a break, and I wondered if she had been in season which could make animals behave very oddly.

Jason said they would get her back to the yard and make sure everything was alright, so we settled in to enjoy the rest of the day.

Chester were fabulous hosts, putting on a three-course carvery with wine, and we made full use of it. Once again, as soon as the race was over, my nerves left me. I was too busy chatting to Charles, Seamus and Ken to bother with many bets, and the ones that I did have did nothing to raise my spirits. However, by the end of the day we had several new friends, some interesting phone numbers, and the confidence that today had been an aberration. Star Of Lady M would be back, but almost certainly not at Chester. Sally even got to chat to Frankie Dettori, so she certainly made the most of the occasion.

Chapter Eighteen

The following day, we received the good news that Star Of Lady M was back at the yard and doing fine. She would have an easy couple of days, and then they would get her back to work. The Marygate was clearly out of the question, so we would have to look at alternatives. Sandown or Beverley at the end of the month were possibilities, with the Sandown race being one that often had a small field despite it being Listed.

As the dust settled, Star Of Lady M was given a TopSpeed of just 40, which emphasised that there must have been something amiss. It is not normal to go from 80 to 40 in just one race. Her RPR of 68 was fair, though again, it showed that we should have beaten the opposition and did not really run our race.

The Racing Post usually gives a good analysis, and in this case, they were concise and to the point. Their opinion that she was soon beaten was absolutely correct.

We are not really in the racehorse ownership world for the prize money. Star Of Lady M had already repaid her purchase price and much of her first-year training fees, but even so, it is always nice to be in the money. At Chester, everyone was guaranteed a payout, and in our case, this amounted to the sixth-place prize of £427.49, return of stakes of £24.76, sponsorship totalling £81, and appearance money of £45.12. We had to pay the entry fee of £192.95 and the jockey fee of £193.97, but even after running badly, she still showed a profit. Of course, that does not take into account our driver, the trainer costs for transport and the stable staff, and the drinks bill in the restaurant, but you probably get the picture.

On a brighter note, Fittleton Ferry was entered into another race, this time at Chepstow. I would not be able to go, but it was something to look forward to.

The buzz of the involvement had become rather addictive, and days when nothing happened, or there were no scheduled runners that I was interested in, became tedious. I analysed every two-year-old race between then and the end of the season, wondering where we might go next. It was easier to imagine races for Emerald Duchess, but for Star Of Lady M, I thought that maybe the race at York in the new Sunday Series might be a consideration, despite having to carry a 10lb penalty. Ultimately, this would need to be discussed with the stable, but the Hilary Needler at Beverley or the National at Sandown were, in my mind, the likelier options.

Confirmation came through that we were not entered in the Marygate, and Jason's assessment was correct, it was a hot race. Carmela and Fix You, the only fillies rated higher than Star Of Lady M after their first race, were both engaged, as was the much improved Primrose Ridge. It would still have been nice to see Star Of Lady M take her chance, but maybe we would have to wait for her three-year-old career to feature at York. Royal Ascot seemed a forlorn hope, but although the pomp and ceremony would contribute to a great day out, I would much prefer our filly to be competitive wherever she races.

Less than a week had passed since the Chester race, but already I was anxious to know of our future plans. Jason admitted that he had not really thought about it, and he was just happy to get her back to her regular work. We had the York Marygate meeting to look forward to, but there were other two-year-old races to keep an eye on. Havana Grey was the leading first season sire; in fact, he was the leading overall sire in some reports. There was also the progress of those that we had beaten at Redcar and Ripon. Could they come out and win, thereby franking the form? Teatime Tipple was entered at Beverley, and he was the favourite. Unfortunately, he played up in the stalls in what looked like a nasty incident. He was withdrawn from the race, and we could only hope that horse and jockey were fine afterwards. It showed just how fragile the sport can be, and we could reflect that our journey had been blessed this far.

Later that day, Fittleton Ferry raced at Chepstow. She was 80/1 for the Class 6 handicap, and was not really given much of a chance. However, no one told the horse that, and she stayed on gamely to get fourth place. The prize was just £349, but it showed clear progression, and hopefully, she would break her maiden before too much longer. As an added bonus, Sky Bet paid four places and so my each-way bet produced a handsome dividend. Her RPR leapt to 53.

I filled in a few idle hours by poring over races. I suggested to Richard Kent and Tim Easterby that Friday 20th May at Haydock might be a good opening for Emerald Duchess, as the race was a maiden fillies contest restricted to bands C and D. In previous seasons, it had cut up to less than ten runners, and it was an EBF qualifier for any horse that finished in the first six. Richard agreed, adding that he thought many of the southern trainers would not fancy heading up the M6 to Haydock on a Friday. Tim said he would see how she was on entries day, which was the following Saturday.

Chapter Nineteen

Star Of Lady M had limited opportunities, with just Musselburgh in a Class 2 contest, as well as the National at Sandown, and the Hilary Needler at Beverley. The Musselburgh race seemed an easy one to dismiss, as it was a long way to go and she would have to carry an 8lb penalty.

By the time the York meeting came around, I had accepted our absence and could remain philosophical about it. I could have a good and relaxing day out, and I could content myself that there was a reasonable excuse as to why she did not perform at Chester. There would have been no such excuse in the Marygate, and there would certainly be no excuse next time she ran.

We headed for York and were delighted to find that Middlethorpe Hall now had the services of a driver. He was there to take guests to and from the course for the same price as a taxi, though we knew that taxis could be difficult to get hold of both before and after racing. So, Terry the driver collected us, and explained that he had been Frankie Dettori's driver for around ten years. That day, he had taken Mrs Dettori to a few designer outlets, and then to other shops to get some nibbles.

Miami Girl was favourite for the Marygate, but she went against all of the statistics that I had researched. Lost Angel and Pillow Talk had finished first and second in the race that saw Emerald Duchess make her debut, and Primrose Ridge would take her place in the line-up. The unbeaten pair Carmela and Fix You were confirmed in the field, though Fix You later became a non-runner.

The race was a good one, with Pillow Talk streaking to a comfortable win, ridden by Danny Tudhope. Primrose Ridge finished sixth, and I could be pleased about that. We had three quarters of a length to spare over Primrose Ridge at Redcar, but that would not have been enough to get us a place at York.

As the afternoon wore on, Sally spotted Terry near the parade ring. He was with Mrs Dettori, and Sally wasted no time in introducing herself. Catherine Dettori was delightful. She had such a friendly manner, and it seemed that Sally and her were about to embark on a long friendship. Unfortunately, Terry and Catherine had to disappear into the parade ring to be with Frankie and the superstar, Stradivarius.

The following day we took the opportunity to visit Star Of Lady M at David O'Meara's as it was less than twenty minutes from our hotel.

I was keeping a close eye on the entries for the Haydock Race, and they quickly went up to ten with at least three more hours before they closed. At the yard we met David's Jack Russell again, as well as Dympna, David's mother. She was a great companion as we waited for the clock to tick around to 9.30, our allotted gallops time. Shortly afterwards, head lad Aaron Bateman came along, followed by Jason Kelly. It was all very relaxed as Jason went to make a cup of tea. It appeared that some of the stable might be a little the worse for wear, after celebrating and commiserating with various owners following a busy three days at York.

We chatted about our filly, and when Sally described the way that she was in the pre-parade ring at Chester, Jason suspected that she could indeed have been in season as we had already suggested. It would not be anyone's intention to structure a racing career around when a filly is in season, but this would likely have been her first season, and therefore she could have been quite upset by it.

Thoughts turned to her next entry as we wandered across to her stable, with Jason happy to consider multiple entries towards the end of the month. He also suggested that we could still go for another novice bonus race, particularly towards the end of the season when they could become weaker. Another possibility was to look for a race similar to the one at Ripon that might come down to a handful of runners, in which case, she could well defy even a hefty penalty.

We also talked about the Marygate, and with Primrose Ridge coming in sixth, it confirmed that we would have had a chance of maybe sneaking into a place, but there were certainly no thoughts that it was a lost opportunity.

Out on the gallops, Star Of Lady M was back to her old self. She cantered up the hill a couple of times, no doubt wondering what all of the fuss was about. David was there, as was Dympna who had taken a shine to Sally, and Char-lee who accompanied the horse to her debut win at Redcar. David was keen to hear Jason's thoughts on entries, and he was definitely in favour of the Hilary Needler. That was two weeks away, but it gave me something to focus on for some more research. The main thing that I discovered was that in general, the first three at Beverley would take their chance at Royal Ascot. So maybe the Royal Meeting was not quite out of the question just yet.

Sally and Dympna were nowhere to be seen as Jason and myself went to see Star Of Lady M get washed down after her exercise. I took a few photos and then said goodbye to Jason. He was off to Dublin for the football semi-final involving his local team, Kildare. Before that, he was accompanying Dympna to the races at Thirsk, and we found Sally and Dympna back at the car. They had talked their way into a lift back from the gallops with Aaron. It had been a chilled out and entertaining morning with no surprises. A morning in which everyone seemed to have the same intention for our horse. She was being treated gently, and it was important that we found a race in which conditions would suit her, both in terms of the course and the opposition.

By the time we got home, there were twenty-four confirmed entries for the Haydock race, a huge amount. However, it would still be a good opportunity to test her over an extra furlong, and at this stage it was still very much about her education. I also got a message from Nikki Evans that Fittleton Ferry was entered into a race at Bath on the same day. That race had thirty-three entries, so it seemed that Friday was a popular day.

On Saturday afternoon, David O'Meara had his second two-year-old winner of the season, when Maria Branwell won at Thirsk ridden by Jason Watson. Danny Tudhope was riding for Godolphin in the Lockinge at Newbury. He finished a good second to the budding superstar, Baaeed.

On Monday morning, plans were thrown into turmoil again. Jason Kelly called to say that he had not entered Star Of Lady M in the Musselburgh race, but he had entered her in a Class 5 contest at Lingfield the following Saturday evening. His rationale was that the race could cut up, and we could offset the 14lb penalty by using a claimer. I was not convinced, and further scrutiny revealed that of the thirteen entries, only four of them had other engagements. It did not look like the race was going to cut up as much as we hoped. In my mind, I had to think of all eventualities. If she won, would she still run at Beverley, or would she go to Royal Ascot as previous winners of the Lingfield race had done? If she lost, would she run in the Hilary Needler, or would we give her an extended break? There were not many other Class 5 races that would be suitable for her.

On the other hand, if she ran in the National and got a place, she would get black type, and would almost certainly be headed for Royal Ascot. However, if the National looked more competitive than usual, then she could still go for the Hilary Needler. Again, if she ran into a place, she would head to Royal Ascot. In either case, if she lost, we would at least be able to gauge what level she could actually perform at. In a Class 5 event at Lingfield, carrying a lot of weight, we would not necessarily learn much.

Meanwhile, as the days went by, the Haydock race for Emerald Duchess was looking slightly better. Just six of the runners plus ourselves did not have other entries. That could optimistically bring the field down to single figures by Friday, though there were more likely to be fourteen or fifteen declarations.

As it turned out, there were ten declared. These included ourselves and Glorious Angel, the horse that ran fourth in the Lily Agnes. So, we would be able to renew acquaintances with Charles Ledigo rather quickly. *Sporting Life* listed Emerald Duchess at 33/1, with Glorious Angel as the favourite. However, we were confident of a better showing given Emerald Duchess's experience, the softer ground, and the extra furlong.

I also got a message that Fittleton Ferry was declared in the first at Bath, another Class 6 handicap with so many runners that it had divided into two. She was also priced at 33/1. Given that she finished fourth last time out, I was encouraged to put an each-way double on the pair.

The Lingfield race was still on the cards for Star Of Lady M, but Lingfield on a Saturday night was not my idea of heaven. However, Jason assured me that we would only go there with a favourite's chance. Of the thirteen entries, one of them ran earlier in the week. Another three were entered in other races, so Jason's assumption that the race might cut up could have been correct. As the declaration stage approached, there were only two other horses that still had alternative engagements. We would have to give 14lbs to Favourite Queen, who had finished third and second, and Lahina Bay, who had finished sixth and third. There was also Byefornow who had won his only race. He would carry a 7lb penalty, but he also had a claimer on board.

It was not looking good, but we would have to see how it panned out the following day. I noticed later that evening that Star Of Lady M had an entry in the Hilary Needler. This could only mean one thing: she was going to be scratched from the Lingfield race.

The next morning, I watched the Lingfield declarations tick up, and when they reached eight, I received the expected call from Jason Kelly. We were not going to Lingfield, but we were entered into the Hilary Needler. Saturday afternoon at Beverley was infinitely preferable to Saturday evening at Lingfield, but now my daily countdown demons could resume. I still suggested that we could enter the National at Sandown to see how it panned out, but I was happy with our current plans. Nine days to go, and in the meantime, there was the small matter of a trip to Haydock Park with Emerald Duchess.

Chapter Twenty

It turned out to be a surprisingly eventful morning on the day of the Haydock race. It is only an hour away from our home, and I spent the early part of the day checking the entries for the National. They soon reached ten, and progressed to twelve, thirteen, fourteen. By the time we arrived at the course it was clear that there were too many, and it was no surprise when Jason messaged to say that there were seventeen entries, including a lot of colts, and we would not be entering. That cleared the way for Beverley and the Hilary Needler the following week, eight days away.

We pulled in to the Owners & Trainers car park at Haydock and found our way to the Owners reception. We had requested two extra badges beyond the allocated eight, as well as two additional luncheon vouchers, and happily these were waiting for us on arrival at a total cost of £45. We went in to the Owners bar, and we were told that the whole of the Owners area was under refurbishment. I did consider that for a prestigious course that had gone through Covid and a sparse winter jumping season, perhaps they could have refurbished in plenty of time for the flat. Regardless, we had some very decent draught Guinness and Pravha, and we watched Fittleton Ferry finish a disappointing twelfth of thirteen at Bath. Her RPR of 10 was about as low as I have ever seen, down from 53 in her previous race. Afterwards, Nikki Evans said that it could have been the ground, or she could perhaps have been in season.

The bar area at Haydock had a huge entrance that was wide open, and the place was cold. So, we moved next door to the dining area. There was a dining room, and an anteroom that contained several high tables close to the bar. These did not look like they were for diners, so we sat there. The dining room organiser said that our tables might be needed if the dining room filled up, so we said that if that happened, we would move. In the meantime, we ordered drinks from a waiter. It was a somewhat frosty reception, made worse when the waiter said that he could not serve us draught beer which was only available at the official Owners bar. The official Owners bar was some twenty feet away, but rather than get into a debate about it, we settled for bottles.

Charles Ledigo said, "Hello", his Glorious Angel had shortened as favourite for Emerald Duchess's race, and then I received an odd email. It said that Emerald Duchess had been entered into a race at Ripon the following Thursday. The entries for the race included Carmela, Breege and Lady Bullet, all operating at well above the standard set so far by Emerald Duchess. By chance, Will Easterby walked in at about the same time, so I asked him about the entry. He had no idea, so we dismissed it and prepared for that afternoon's race.

Emerald Duchess looked very well in the paddock, and Duran Fentiman was again on board. Both Will and Duran were managing our expectations, looking for a clear progression and perhaps passing a few more runners with a late surge. As it turned out, quite the opposite happened. We made our way to the viewing area, where the winning line was at a surprising angle. By the end of the race this did not really bother us. Emerald Duchess missed the break, though not as badly as at Nottingham, but then showed an effortless burst to move into a challenging position. By half way, she was amongst the leaders, but she then faded quite dramatically. When we spoke to Duran afterwards, he said that this might be due to missing some work with sore shins, but also that the ground was on the firm side again and she was fighting against it. However, he was impressed with her early speed that saw her overcome a slow break, even suggesting that she might revert back to five furlongs.

She finished eighth of the ten runners, well in touch with the few in front of her, and it was not too much of a disappointment. Her RPR of 47 was an improvement from her previous mark of 41, though her TopSpeed went down from 39 to 37. However, I had yet to find anyone who understood what TopSpeed is or took much notice of it. Charles Ledigo was a little subdued after Glorious Angel could only finish fourth.

Will bought us drinks in the bar, and we had a good chat about Maryland, where he had ridden in the Maryland Hunt Cup. We discussed various other parts of the US, as well as cricket. Emerald Duchess got a mention, but we all knew she needed a bit more time. She had already run twice before the end of May, which was way beyond expectations, especially when you considered that her sire, Massaat, did not run until July in his two-year-old year, and he only ran three times in that season overall.

After the race, I had conversations with Richard Kent and Luke Lillingston. Both were very impressed with the speed that Emerald Duchess showed to make up the ground lost at the break, with Luke stating that she had clearly got talent. They accepted that the ground was once again against her, and that often Haydock's ground is not quite as described by the official Clerk of the Course. The following day it was no surprise to find that she once again had a sore shin, but she was well in herself.

Chapter Twenty-One

The entries for Beverley would not be published until Monday, so it would be a long weekend of waiting. I was actually busy on the Monday morning helping my wife catalogue the local graveyard. In between finding names of the long since departed, I refreshed the BHA entries screen. The numbers seemed to be increasing quite rapidly, but eventually they stopped at eighteen. When they were officially published, I took a glance down them. It was a competitive race. Miami Girl, favourite for the Marygate, was in there, as were Beautiful Eyes, Lost Angel, Primrose Ridge and Shandy Star, who all finished in the top ten at York. There were four unbeaten fillies, including the Lily Agnes winner, Absolutelyflawless, and there was even an entry from Aidan O'Brien.

Monday night was spent analysing the race further, in terms of other entries. Three of the higher rated fillies were entered into the National on Thursday, and several more at Pontefract on the Friday. Altogether, seven of the eighteen had alternative engagements.

On Tuesday, the National declarations were published, and none of the three filles were declared to run. We were still very likely to have a dozen or more runners at Beverley, making the draw very important. By my estimate, we would be about sixth in the betting. I started to look at other races that might be suitable if she did not do well at Beverley, but with two wins the penalties were hefty. Windsor on 25th June was a possibility, as she would only have a 5lb penalty, and there were often just a few runners in that contest. There was some good news, in that Danny Tudhope was listed as our jockey for the Hilary Needler.

On Wednesday, the Pontefract race had cut up badly with just four declarations, none of which were originally entered in the Hilary

Needler. However, two runners were declared at Carlisle and Haydock on Friday, which effectively cut the Hilary Needler down to sixteen. Later that day, two more runners were entered for races the following Tuesday, which probably meant we could cut our entries down to a maximum of fourteen.

By coincidence, there was a meeting at Beverley that same afternoon, and disaster struck when it had to be abandoned after just four races. The bottom bend was considered to be dangerous, though assurances were given that it would be fine for Saturday. The Hilary Needler is a straight five furlongs, and so would not be affected by the bottom bend, but there was a danger that the entire fixture could be cancelled. Although this was unlikely, I checked out where else we might go, other than Royal Ascot. York on 10th June was about the most appealing. It was a fillies-only Class 3 contest, and we would have to carry a 10lb penalty.

I awaited the release of the declarations on Thursday morning with great interest. I watched the BHA declarations list from around 8.30am, with the deadline being 10am. Jason Kelly called and said there is no reason not to enter, a somewhat negative slant but one which I fully understood. I was expecting around twelve declarations, but when the final list was published there were just nine, and several of the big players had not declared. These included the probable favourite, Beautiful Eyes, as well as Aidan O'Brien's Deneuve. We were up against Absolutelyflawless again, as well as Primrose Ridge. Parr Fire and Fragrance were two other previous winners, and Richard Hannon was represented by Distinguished Lady.

David O'Meara also ran the debutant, Your Spirit, but we had secured the services of stable jockey, Danny Tudhope. The draw at Beverley is not as significant as Chester, but getting the number four berth was a small win as the higher numbers are described as being "out in the car park". *Sporting Life* initially listed us at 8/1, but I doubted whether that price would hold with the actual bookmakers.

The day before the race, there appeared to be money for Richard Hannon's Distinguished Lady. Although still a maiden, she was challenging Absolutelyflawless for favouritism. The same analyst who wrote "judged on breeding others are more appealing" about Star Of Lady M before her debut at Redcar, now suggested, "disappointing when taken on for the lead in the Lily Agnes 24 days ago". She was clearly not fancied, but there were some crumbs of comfort on Twitter. Avid two-year-old student Mike Curtis wrote, "Happy to put a line through Star Of Lady M run at Chester, I think she's the best in here and she can reverse the 4 1/2 lengths (from the Lily Agnes)."

The most disappointing comment I heard came in a podcast. Trainer Darryl Holland, whose Primrose Ridge had finished second to Star Of Lady M back at Redcar, said that the Redcar defeat was purely down to the ground, and Star Of Lady M would never beat his filly again. I thought that it was a little disrespectful towards our girl, but I guess he was being interviewed and had to think of something to say.

Chapter Twenty-Two

Distinguished Lady was clear favourite overnight, whilst we were around 8/1. As the morning progressed, Absolutelyflawless came back in to head the market, and we shortened to 7/1. We prepared for the almost two-hour drive to Beverley, but at least it was Saturday, and the traffic would probably be light. Our two sons, Ole and Zachary, got into a panic trying to find shirts, shoes and ties that were only purchased in February. As well as Ole and Zachary, we had Ole's girlfriend, Abbie, as the fifth member of our party. We set off for the course, taking the scenic route to Sheffield before hitting three motorways. It was uneventful until someone decided that the M62 would be better as a single lane rather than three, and that delayed us for around half an hour.

We parked up next to Mick Fitzgerald who was busy studying form, and then we went to the Owners & Trainers reception to collect our badges. We were greeted with a glass of champagne, and our badges were adorned with a union jack in honour of the Very British Racing Day. This was coincidentally appropriate as I wore my red, white and blue striped blazer. The Owners & Trainers section was quite spacious, with a nice terrace outside that was unfortunately too cold to sit at. I paced nervously around it, and distracted myself by talking to some other owners who had travelled across from Cumbria.

The boys had been to Galway races previously, but that was seated at a table overlooking the winning line and betting exclusively on the Tote. They had also been to Southwell many years before, but the most memorable thing about that was Zac staring incredulously at the diminutive jockeys and asking, "They let kids do this?" I showed them around the betting ring, the parade ring and the viewing area, and they decided to use the Tote for convenience. After a brief pause whilst they retrieved their IDs to prove their ages, they had a bet in the first and we went into the stands to watch. Zac backed the first winner at 6/1 and had the second each-way at 80/1, whilst Ole backed the second each-way. So, they were both off to a fine start. It is always good to see some familiar faces at the racetrack, and we were pleased to bump into Will Easterby who wished us good luck. Neil and Lesley Thornton also came along to support us, and they too had a favourable result in the first race, but now it was time for Star Of Lady M.

In no time at all our filly was in the pre-parade ring. She was a little on her toes, but nowhere near as bad as at Chester. She made her way to the parade ring, and I followed her in along with Sally. I beckoned to the other three and Ole joined us, but Zac and Abbie seemed a little intimidated by the prospect of crossing the path that the horses were walking around on. Things were happening quickly, and I felt like I had my nerves under control.

David O'Meara was in attendance along with Char-lee Heard, and they were very relaxed. David introduced us to the owners of his second horse in the race, and then Danny came out resplendent in the emerald green silks with the bold black stars. I asked him about tactics but he was not giving anything away. "We'll just see how the race pans out" was about as detailed as he got, and in my mind, I wondered whether this was confidence or nerves.

Star Of Lady M now had a groom on her inside as well as her outside, and this calmed her down significantly. Danny mounted, and they were off to the start. We went into the grandstand where we could see the big screen opposite, as well as having a great view down the course. The nerves really began to churn. My throat was dry as I considered what a good result would be after the disaster of Chester. First six would guarantee a prize. Second or third would mean a conversation about Royal Ascot. A win would be out of this world, and would include a third GBB.

She went into stall four very calmly, despite the newcomer, Your Spirit, playing up at the post. Eventually, they were all in, and they were off. She dived left at the start, but showed good pace to fall in just behind Mark Johnston's Fragrance. Primrose Ridge came from the outside at a blistering pace and soon took the lead. We passed Fragrance and tracked the leader. After a couple of furlongs, it was clear that she was a very different filly to the one at Chester. With two and a half to go, Primrose Ridge was going further clear, but we were holding second. The rest of the field were struggling as we passed the two-furlong pole, and the thought of finishing second, that had seemed so appealing before the race, was now possibly a disappointment.

A furlong and a half out, we were probably two lengths down, but Jack Mitchell on board the leader had gone for his whip. Passing the furlong pole, there was still clear daylight between the two, but Danny then urged our girl for an effort. She responded, cutting into the lead, but she was still a length down with half a furlong left to race. He drove her harder, and she picked up. She was gaining. Would the post come too soon? She was flying, and in the split second it took me to switch my eyes from the screen to the live action, she had gained half a length. Beverley is a stiff uphill track, and the finish can be gruelling after a hard race, but Star was loving it. Her ears were pricked as the commentator called, "Primrose Ridge being mowed down by Star Of Lady M". She put her head in front, then effortlessly eased to victory by three quarters of a length, the same distance that she had beaten the same rival at Redcar.

The last hundred yards were all heart, and the deficit from three quarters down to three quarters up was in the blink of an eye.

She won going away from Primrose Ridge, with the rest a few lengths further back. Sally's hat went up into the air, the boys and Abbie were buzzing, and then they announced that they had all backed her. As soon as she crossed the finishing line my nerves evaporated, but the adrenaline did not. I rushed to the parade ring amongst congratulations from many of the Beverley racegoers. Danny had dismounted and was about to be interviewed. "Put a line through Chester and she's unbeaten," he said, and followed this up with, "She deserves her chance at Royal Ascot." David suggested, "The owners might want to go to Royal Ascot," and he was also quick to dismiss the Chester race. Mick Fitzgerald had a brief word with us and then it was time for the presentation.

We received our wonderful trophy from a relative of the original Hilary Needler. We were then asked several questions about what went wrong at Chester and whether we would go to Royal Ascot. Sally said that if we were going there, she would need a helicopter. David received a trainer's trophy, and then Danny received a bag as the winning jockey. Beverley are quite rightly proud of their race; the Hilary Needler is synonymous with the course. It is a Class 2 race, but it used to be Listed, and I am sure that they would love to see the Listed status restored. We were led away to a presentation room, where a large television was already showing reruns of the race. There were so many people in there that I thought they must be connections of all of the other horses. We spoke to the Chairman of the course and various other dignitaries, and they were all urging us to head not just for Royal Ascot but for the Group 2 Queen Mary. They were genuinely wishing us well, but there was also the slightly hidden agenda that if our horse did well at Royal Ascot, it would go some way to proving that the Hilary Needler once again deserved to be Listed. Very shortly afterwards, Beverley Racecourse followed me on Twitter.

Go Racing In Yorkshire were quickly up to speed, tweeting about another step forward for a potential "Yorkshire Wonder Horse". Three down and six to go, but it would still be a virtually impossible task.

I had to be careful with the champagne due to having a long drive home, so we said our thanks and headed back to the Owners & Trainers area. As ever, my phone had exploded with messages. I got through them, and then the phone calls began. First up it was Luke, and he was thrilled with her performance. He did throw a bit of a curveball at us by suggesting that rather than heading for Royal Ascot we could go to France. Across the Channel, we could pick up a Listed race with very decent prize money, as these tended to be weaker than over here. There was also a message from Whitsbury Manor suggesting that the Empress Stakes at Newmarket would be a good option, but that was six furlongs and David had confirmed that for now she would stick to five. They also advised against Royal Ascot as it can ruin a horse, and we did not want another Chester on our hands.

Back down to earth, we realised that the debate about whether she would be rated 75 or 95 had been settled in our favour. We had also won the £20,000 prize as well as the £20,000 GBB. Congratulations came from all angles, with many of the locals keen to share their memories of the Hilary Needler. It really was a proud moment to now be a part of that history. I chatted to people too numerous to mention, and I think that our appeal was that we were not one of the big players, we were just ordinary people enjoying the thrill of owning our first racehorse.

The boys were almost in shock. Ole, like me, thought that with a furlong to go she was not going to win, and that burst of acceleration was really something. They got back to betting, but several races went by without me taking much notice of them.

The general consensus was that we had to go to Royal Ascot. We might never get the chance again, but that decision would have to wait. An hour or so later, the colts ran for a similar trophy to ours, and Mike Curtis messaged me to say that our winning time was faster than theirs, another small achievement. Will Easterby passed on his congratulations, and then we joined Neil and Lesley Thornton for a drink in one of the grandstand bars. Unfortunately, Sally was unable to get champagne and so had to make do with a gin and tonic, but she still had a full bottle waiting for her back at our table.

We had enjoyed another thrilling day, perhaps the best yet, and we headed for home. The journey back was mercifully quick, and we strolled to the Drum & Monkey for our traditional post-race celebration. We went to Whaley Bridge Bowling Club, which was in the midst of the Champions League final, but well-wishers came from everywhere. Most of them had backed her again, some had won more than others, and some were just happy for us. If our local bookie was still around, he would definitely have gone bust after our win.

I returned home around 1am and of course, turned the television on, retrieved the USB, and watched the race several more times. I then watched the ITV coverage that I had recorded, where Jason Weaver was the only one who gave Star Of Lady M a chance, before finally falling into bed.

The next day, I concentrated on all of the Twitter messages, including an interesting follow from Jamie Osborne. I wondered if he was regretting missing out on the purchase, or whether he had forgotten all about it and was just genuinely interested.

I had a call with Richard Kent who urged me to take our filly to Royal Ascot. He asked me if I had any intention of selling her at the London sale, and as I had never heard of the London sale, and I had no intention of selling her, I said "No." He told me that he goes to too many funerals where the deceased has never really had any major milestones in their life, and this was an opportunity that might never happen again. Richard can get a bit carried away, often in jest, but this time he was absolutely right. He also suggested that a reasonable figure for insurance purposes would be around £150,000, so that was added to my "To Do" list.

Jason messaged me to tell me that Star Of Lady M had come out of the race absolutely fine, and we would have a call the following day to discuss options. I passed the time by creating a new ringtone, so now when anyone calls, I will hear "Primrose Ridge being mowed down by Star Of Lady M. Star Of Lady M's won the Hilary Needler."

Chapter Twenty-Three

On Sunday evening, I spoke to Luke, and in a way, it defined the future for myself, Sally, and Star Of Lady M. He told me that David O'Meara had called him and advised, in the nicest way, that the best thing to do now was to sell her. He did not want to lose her from the yard, but it was his job to maximise potential. She clearly had the ability to go to Royal Ascot, and there were a lot of people who would pay a lot of money to have such a runner. The London sale mentioned by Richard was on the Monday of Royal Ascot week, and that is where we could expect to collect at least six figures for her. Basically, at that moment in time she was probably as valuable as she was ever likely to get, entirely because of Royal Ascot.

An alternative route would be to keep her to eventually become a broodmare. To do that, we needed to seek out a black type race as soon as possible, and even though Royal Ascot would provide such an opportunity, the chances of finishing in the first three were actually quite remote. I did check out ante-post betting on the Queen Mary, and Star Of Lady M was in there at 40/1, alongside Absolutelyflawless that we had just beaten. Perhaps they had not updated their odds yet?

Luke was not advising one way or the other, because he obviously knew that we were on a journey, and that he had helped to set us off down this path. As a professional in the industry, he would definitely sell. It was quite possible that Star Of Lady M had reached her potential, and that it would be all downhill from here. The fact that her sire won a Group 1 race in his second racing season was irrelevant. There was certainly a chance that his daughter was a good, precocious filly that had reached her peak. I preferred to consider the impact of her sire, who was also a precocious two-year-old that extended his success as a three-year-old.

It was all explained in simple and clear terms, for which I will always be grateful to Luke and David, but did I have a decision to make? I explained the situation to Sally, and to the boys. They were all still on a high from Beverley, and twenty-four hours later might we be considering a sale? I said we were not, but Sally suggested that £400,000 might be a figure that would be worth taking. I shook my head.

As I mulled it over, I had already made up my mind. I just had to consider how best to phrase my intention.

Ultimately, the desire for so many people to spend considerable sums of money to have a runner at Royal Ascot emphasised just how elite it is, and to be able to genuinely own such a runner should be seen as a privilege. As you will know by now, I am an avid user of the BHA race search website, and I had mapped out the Queen Mary, the Dragon Stakes at Sandown or the Duchess of Cambridge at Newmarket, possibly Glorious Goodwood, but definitely either the Lowther or more likely, the Julia Graves at York. I had not gone into September; I did not want to get too far ahead of myself.

Simon Chappell popped up in my messages, and he was in no doubt that we should head for the Queen Mary. He also largely agreed with all of my other suggestions, particularly the Julia Graves. York remains our favourite course, and so while we had the chance to race there, we simply had to take it. Although I had no regrets about heading to the Lily Agnes rather than the Marygate, the Ebor meeting at the Knavesmire in August was not going to be missed.

So, armed with that information, I tried to explain as best as I could to Luke.

"Thanks for the call last night. Really helped to clarify our position in my mind as I consider all possibilities. You know our situation. We didn't do this to make millions, or even to get our money back. We did it for the experience. It's a real rollercoaster and it's our rollercoaster. Totally understand and appreciate David's call to you - he would not be doing his job if he was not trying to maximise her potential. She might never win another race again, but I'm convinced that her racing career will be wholly adorned by the emerald green with black stars. We're not expecting to win at Royal Ascot, but if by some chance we sold her and she did win, then the regret would be off the charts. I've not spoken to Jason yet, but I'm almost convinced we should head to Royal Ascot then look at maybe the Dragon at Sandown or one of the smaller group races, then the Julia Graves at York (or the Lowther, but that might be a step too far). And at some point, we'd like you to be there with us. And anyway, I can't sell her yet - the book about our story would not be long enough."

It was a relief when I had written the words and sent the message. I was definitely right about one thing, if we had sold her and she had won at Royal Ascot, those regrets would haunt me forever. I do not think that I would be very popular in the village either. Judging by their reaction after the Beverley win, it seemed like it was their journey too.

The TopSpeed rating of 66 from the Beverley race was a little disappointing, especially as she had reached 80 at Ripon. However, as I have said before no one that I have asked really understands what that is, so I did not let it worry me. Her RPR improved to 88, up five points on Ripon, but still not quite at the levels of the favourites for the races at Ascot.

Chapter Twenty-Four

The following morning, I had the chance to mull over the past forty-eight hours, and what it actually meant. I was almost certain that whenever Star Of Lady M raced, she would carry the distinctive emerald green with black stars. Even when she reached the broodmare stage, we may decide to keep the foal, though that would be far less certain.

Jason let me know that we could agree race plans around 2pm, after he had sorted the weekend entries. That was then delayed until 3pm to give him a chance to analyse the options, and in particular, the results of Hilary Needler winners at the Royal Meeting. It seemed like a very long wait. It was actually around 3.20pm when we got to chat, and Jason explained our options very clearly and concisely. The Norfolk Stakes would probably be a step too far in terms of quality, and there was no sense in increasing her distance to six furlongs just yet. That left the Queen Mary and the Windsor Castle. The Queen Mary is a Group 2 race for fillies only. It also has the advantage of being the first race on the card. The Windsor Castle is a Listed race open to colts and fillies, and takes place more than three hours later. Would my nerves be able to stand that wait? Wesley Ward, the famous American trainer, had what he considered the best horse he had ever sent to Royal Ascot entered in the Queen Mary. This could put off a lot of potential challengers. On the other hand, the very best fillies would go for the Queen Mary and therefore we might have a better chance in the Windsor Castle.

I almost had to pinch myself during the conversation. There were no other options, just the two races on the same day at Royal Ascot. So, we were definitely going. In the end, we decided to enter both races and see how they panned out at the declarations stage. That was perhaps a little extravagant in terms of entry fees, but she had earned the right to have the options. We were really using the Royal Ascot entry as an experience, as opposed to a genuine chance of winning, and as long as Star Of Lady M was happy and came away none the worse for her experience, I was OK with that.

We also discussed what might happen after Royal Ascot, and it was black type all the way. The Dragon was a possibility, and there were races at Newmarket and Newbury before the Julia Graves Roses at York, but there would be time to discuss that in more detail afterwards.

I then started to let everyone know, and the social media world erupted. I thanked Richard for his advice, and then I spoke to Luke who was as excited as anyone about the decision. I mentioned the Wesley Ward hotpot, but Luke dismissed that with, "he claims to have one of those every year." I invited him to join us at Ascot, but he had a prior lunch engagement with the Ascot Authorities, the people who control the racing at the Royal Meeting. He assured me that he and Tabitha would join us in the parade ring. Incredible, unbelievable, staggering, the superlatives kept on coming. We were heading for Royal Ascot, and we would be one of the cheapest horses there. We were both delighted for each other.

Luke had also spoken to David O'Meara again, and David was very pleased with our decision. He agreed with Luke's suggestion that there might be some Listed races in France that we could aim for, and the prospect of a few days in Paris became a reality.

The next few hours were spent researching the dress code for the Queen Anne Enclosure, and finding quotes for helicopter prices. We could not simply turn up to Royal Ascot in a taxi.

I asked Russell Wild, the chairman of Whaley Bridge Cricket Club, if we could land on the cricket pitch. He not only agreed, he insisted, and stated that our return would involve a reception party.

Prices ranged from £3,000 to more than £13,000, and I am not entirely sure of the reasons behind the differences. I decided to leave it to the following day, and I went to bed with the countdown firmly in progress. There were sixteen days until our big date with Royal Ascot.

I considered that £100,000 would be sufficient for insurance, especially as if she did well at Royal Ascot, we would have to change it again. I contacted James Denley, our insurance man who had taken a keen interest in the career of Star Of Lady M, and he was happy to increase the coverage. I then contacted the yard to get a veterinary certificate.

Meanwhile, the helicopter responses continued to vary wildly. Our best quote came in at just over £4,000, but there was a problem. The six-seater helicopter had a maximum passenger capacity of 450 kilos, and we weighed in at approximately 530 kilos. Now, I do not think that 530 kilos is excessive for six grown adults, at less than 90 kilos each. The helicopter company asked if we could double check the weights, and although there might have been scope to lose a kilo here and there, to bring it down by 80 full kilos would take something as drastic as amputation. They did have a bigger six-seater helicopter, but that came in at more than £12,000.

I figured that two smaller ones would be cheaper than one large one, so we came to a compromise. For £7,500 plus VAT we could get two helicopters that would accommodate all six of us between them. There was myself and Sally, of course, as well as our two sons, Ole and Zachary, and our daughter, Gabriella. Finally, there was my sister, Fiona, and we were all very excited.

I went into Manchester to order some smart navy tails with a stone waistcoat, whilst the girls thumbed through endless options for suitable attire. The boys decided that they would use their existing suits as they could not be bothered with the rigmarole of formal dress. Fortunately, we were in the Queen Anne Enclosure, where the dress code is considerably less formal than the Royal Enclosure.

I received notification that Fittleton Ferry was due to race again, this time at Chepstow the following Saturday. Another five-furlong Class 6 race, for which she was around 16/1. I made a mental note to watch out for that, but I had other things to think about. Simon Chappell messaged me as he had a gazebo within the Royal Enclosure. He advised that the majority of men in the Owners & Trainers would be in top hat and tails, so I decided that my tails would definitely need to be finished off with a topper.

We agreed that we should meet up, though I wondered if Royal Ascot was similar to other racecourses where you could venture into any enclosure up to the status of your ticket. That meant that he would be able to come to the Queen Anne Enclosure but we would not be able to enter the Royal Enclosure.

By Wednesday, with two weeks to go until the big day, several people were asking the question about which race we would be in. The BHA racing administration site was updated with entries into the Queen Mary and Windsor Castle, which was another confirmation that this was really happening. The bookmakers responded by adding Star Of Lady M to their lists. Most of them quoted her at 20/1 or 25/1 for the Queen Mary, with Paddy Power being the exception at 40/1. Wesley Ward's Love Reigns was still the hot favourite, as short as 9/4 in some places. The Windsor Castle was almost ignored, with only Unibet listing her at 20/1.

The following day, there was welcome news related to Emerald Duchess. Her sire, Massaat, had his first winner when Mascapone, who had finished fourth in the Brocklesby, won at Chelmsford. The Brocklesby form was certainly working out well, and Star Of Lady M had already beaten three of the runners.

The Royal Ascot owner registration was open, so I registered us for the Queen Mary, assuming that I would be able to change this if we opted for the Windsor Castle.

That weekend, it was the Jubilee celebration, and Whaley Bridge Cricket Club hosted a major event for the village. As is tradition, I spent most of my time in the bar, serving rather than drinking, and so met a great many people. Everyone was interested, including some people that I had never met. The legend of Star Of Lady M was growing almost daily. The helicopter ride to and from Royal Ascot would only add to that legend regardless of the result.

It was also the weekend of the Oaks and the Derby, and I managed to pick the wrong horse in both races. Fittleton Ferry finished a disappointing seventh at Chepstow, with the explanation that perhaps she needed further and a stronger ride from her jockey. It seemed that the trainer may be going down a previously trodden path, and perhaps the horse was simply not cut out to be a racehorse. She was entered again at Chepstow the following week, but it was doubtful that she would run.

Chapter Twenty-Five

For the first time in many weeks, the next step for Star Of Lady M was clearly defined and unlikely to change. We still had to decide on which race she would run in, but we knew we were going to be at Royal Ascot on the Wednesday. There was little to speculate on, but I did put my mind to where she might go after Ascot. I was very familiar with the choices in the UK, but Luke and David were both thinking that France might be a better option to pick up some black type. She could achieve this with a top three finish at Ascot, but it is always good to have a back-up plan. Deauville seemed to be the most likely destination on 10th July, but it was not an easy place to get to. I did some research, but with so many unknowns, I decided to leave it for a later date. Perhaps we should just pin our hopes on winning the Queen Mary and then we could remain in the UK.

With a week to go, the next milestone would be the entries for the Coventry Stakes, the only two-year-old race on the first day of the Royal Meeting. They would not be published until 12 noon, so I took the opportunity to go to my local Tesco. It was relatively quiet, but then I bumped into an old friend who asked about Star Of Lady M. One of the shop assistants overheard us. She knew Sally, and she wanted to know all about our racehorse, having heard about it through another friend. She said that she did not normally have a bet, but she would be putting some money on her at Royal Ascot. As I stood by the mangoes, a few more people were showing an interest, and my five-minute shopping trip approached half an hour. One woman said, "I will have to get my son to put a bet on as I don't know how to do it." It seemed that we had created our own version of the Grand National, with Star Of Lady M carrying the weight of many small bets on her big day. I urged caution, and emphasised that there would be many other opportunities, but I sensed that this was not what people wanted to hear. Eventually I got to continue my shopping, check out and return home. As it turned out I had forgotten the mangoes.

News of Star Of Lady M's success was not restricted to these shores. She had already had a tweet about her victories in Arabic, and now she was also headline news in India. However, they did not quite get the translation right as their headline referred to "Star Of Girl M".

The Coventry Stakes entries came out, and three of the first five in the Windsor Castle betting were on the list. There were no fillies, which meant that there was no impact on the Queen Mary. As I looked down the entries for both the Queen Mary and Windsor Castle, I wondered where we might hold an edge. Of course, experience is a big thing for two-year-olds, and as we had already raced four times, we were ahead of the curve. Many of the market leaders had got to their position on the back of a single race, usually when they had won by a significant margin. Whilst this might seem impressive, it also meant that they had not yet been in the heat of battle, and we knew from both Redcar and Beverley that our girl would respond when the chips were down. I was grasping at these positives, or was I clutching at straws? Time would tell.

The entries were finally released and there were thirty in the Queen Mary and forty in the Windsor Castle. Both races had a maximum field size of twenty-eight, so there was a possibility that some horses could be balloted out. I was pleased to see that we were not on the ballot lists, which are based on rating. Of course, we could not run in both, so we had to figure out which would be our best option. Only one filly had been placed in the past ten years in the Windsor Castle, so that seemed like a real long shot. In its favour, that filly had been trained by David O'Meara. It was also true that not many fillies actually ran in the Windsor Castle. It was usually no more than two or three each year, further skewing the stats.

The Queen Mary was slightly more favourable, with two Hilary Needler winners placed in the past six or seven years, and as there was only one Hilary Needler each year, that looked like a more favourable trend. I had a call with Jason Kelly who admitted that it was still a coin toss, though he was leaning towards the Windsor Castle. We discussed jockeys, as Danny Tudhope had already been claimed to ride Dramatised in the Queen Mary and Edgar Linton in the Windsor Castle. We thought that we might want to reserve a jockey for the Windsor Castle, as most of the top riders were already booked up. In the Queen Mary the likes of Frankie Dettori and Ryan Moore were still available. Jason said that he would contact the agents of Tom Marquand, who was third in the jockeys' championship, and Kieran Shoemark, who had ridden a two-year-old winner for David O'Meara the previous day.

There was good news from Tim Easterby that Emerald Duchess was now cantering again, and he would look for another race for her when the ground softened. Meanwhile, Royal Ascot probably had more preview shows than Cheltenham. I consumed them all, though Star Of Lady M was not given a mention. In fact, most of the two-year old-analysis was restricted to Aidan O'Brien's horses and the Wesley Ward hotpot, Love Reigns. This was probably down to so many of them having multiple entries, but it was beginning to become clearer in my mind which juveniles were being earmarked for which races.

In the Queen Mary betting, we were 40/1 with Paddy Power but generally around 25/1 with most other bookmakers. It appeared that the top ten in the betting would all be declared to run, thereby ensuring the quality expected and assumed in a Group 2 race. In the

Windsor Castle, we were 33/1 with Coral but generally around 20/1 elsewhere. I considered that perhaps half of the top ten in the betting would be declared to run, with several alternative targets for the other leading contenders. The favourite for the Windsor Castle was another strong candidate from Aidan O'Brien, but beyond that, if my assumption on runners was correct, all of the next best were rated within four points of each other. That included ourselves.

I noticed that Chateau, a colt that was to be ridden by William Buick, was around 10/1 in the Windsor Castle betting. The interesting thing to note here was that Chateau won the two-year-old race for colts at Beverley on the same day that we won the Hilary Needler. The times were almost identical, although we were very slightly quicker. On that day at Beverley, we carried the same weight, but at Ascot, we would get a 5lb allowance, another advantage of the Windsor Castle over the Queen Mary.

The Albany entries had very little impact on our potential targets, and when the Coventry declarations were in, there was only Paddy's Day that was declared and that we could therefore scratch from the Windsor Castle list.

On Sunday evening, with just three days to go, I had a call with Luke. He gave no more advice regarding which race we should enter, but he did suggest that we might consider Colin Keane, the Irish champion jockey, if we opted for the Windsor Castle. Colin was already booked for Grand Oak in the Queen Mary. I passed the message on to Jason, and awaited the next morning with interest.

With two days to go, we had to declare. Jason spent the early part of the morning contacting jockeys' agents to firm up potential bookings, and he said he would call closer to the declarations cut off time at 10am. Nerves were beginning to fray as the clocked ticked on, and I could always envisage the nightmare scenario where he was about to push the button when there was a power cut, or his laptop crashed, or Windows decided to do one of its interminable updates. I am sure that the arrangements are done much more professionally than that, with all eventualities covered, but demons will be demons.

By 9.30am, we had still not declared, and there were a lot of people wanting to know our final choice, including me. Finally, the call came through with around twenty minutes to spare. It was a brief discussion, and we both agreed that the Windsor Castle would give us our best chance. Colin Keane was secured as our jockey, and I began to let people know. Strangely enough, at around 9.55am we lost all power including WIFI and 4G. So, if I was still waiting to make the entries, I would have failed.

I tried to change our Royal Ascot Owners accreditation from the Queen Mary to the Windsor Castle, but the website would not allow it. I called them, but they were understandably busy, so I emailed them.

Opinions were flying in from all over, but it was generally accepted that we had made the right choice. The only issue was that the Windsor Castle was the sixth race on the card, a full six and a half hours after we were due to arrive at the course. My nerves could well be in tatters by then, or worse: I could have spent too much time in the bar.

The draw came out and we were given the number 1 stall, with the favourite drawn alongside us in stall 2. Not ideal as there is supposedly a slight bias in favour of high numbers at Ascot, and with twenty-four runners, that made it even worse. However, I was reminded that last year's winner, Chipotle, came out of stall 1, so perhaps lightning could strike twice.

The betting still had us at 20/1 up to 33/1, but the RPR had us at joint third best, and TopSpeed had us as joint first. I contacted Royal Ascot Owners & Trainers again to switch us from the Queen Mary to the Windsor Castle. At most courses this would not matter; she was still entered in a race on the same day, but at Royal Ascot, the parade ring passes are issued on a race-by-race basis. They assured me that if I had emailed, they would certainly deal with it. Suitably reassured, I decided to go for a long walk to clear my head, and while I was out, I received a notification that Emerald Duchess had been entered at Pontefract the following Sunday. She was one of twenty-five entries, but the ground was Good to Firm and there was no forecast of rain, so it seemed unlikely that she would run.

For the next day or so I could relax. Well, after I had watched replays of the last few runnings of the Windsor Castle to see how the race panned out. Despite the victory of Chipotle from the same stall as ourselves, it definitely had the feeling of a lottery.

The day before our trip was quite a busy one. I had to go into Manchester to pick up my suit, whilst back at home Sally, Fiona and Gabi discussed outfits and accessories with the weather turning almost tropical. It was also the first day of the Royal Meeting, so we scoured the television to get a sense of the different enclosures and the styles being worn.

The pundits were optimistic, ranging from "Clearly wasn't 100% at Chester and unbeaten aside from that, finding plenty for third win in the Hilary Needler at Beverley 18 days ago. Well worth a shot at this level." to "Didn't take to Chester in the Lily Agnes on her penultimate start but has won her other three outings, including a valuable conditions event at Beverley last time. Needs more but she looks a tough sort and cannot be dismissed easily."

Elsewhere, Emerald Duchess was number four on the elimination sequence for the race at Pontefract, and the weather forecast had changed to indicate a weekend of rain. My instinct was that she would be declared, and then the yard would wait until Sunday morning to make a final decision. Last year, the race divided into two, which would be the best option. Meanwhile, Fittleton Ferry was given an entry at Chepstow for the following Monday. These were interesting notes, but really just a distraction from the main event.

The helicopter company caused a bit of a panic when they said that they had not received landing permission for our trip to Ascot. Fortunately, they were only concerned about the Whaley Bridge Cricket Club end of the journey, which was easily resolved. I had also not heard back from Ascot Owners & Trainers with regard to my request to switch Star Of Lady M badges from the Queen Mary to the Windsor Castle, despite two emails and a number of fruitless phone calls. That would have to be a job for the following morning. My nerves were bad enough without having to tie up several loose ends.

Twitter was very kind to us, with lots more follows and good wishes. For now, we were the pride of Yorkshire, ironic given my cricketing and footballing allegiance to Old Trafford.

We were to carry number 22 in the race, and clutching at straws, I discovered that the number twenty-two represents your angel's way of telling you that you are on the right track and that your dreams are about to become a reality. You will have probably gathered that I was doing just about anything to pass the time.

Bradsell won the first two-year-old race at Royal Ascot, a cheap 12,000 guineas purchase as a yearling. He was drawn in stall 2, although he did track over to the other side of the course. However, it did give me confidence that a horse could win from anywhere if it was good enough and got the run of the race.

Chapter Twenty-Six

On the morning of our race, I decided to embrace the luck of the Irish with a small glass of Irish whiskey. It seemed to work, as I finally got through to Ascot to confirm that race switch, and the helicopter pilot rang me to say they were all on time and expected to land at 9.30am. I said we were booked for 9.40am but that did not seem to bother him, it all seemed very relaxed.

I also received a picture message from David O'Meara showing Star Of Lady M in her Ascot stable. She had her head over the door looking to see what was going on, seemingly unconcerned about the drama that was about to unfold.

Ole was in a grumpy mood, as the girls were up early and still trying on outfits. Eventually, they appeared into the bright sunlight looking radiant. A last-minute sewing job ensured that Gabi's cleavage was not too revealing, and we were ready to go. It was already hot, and as we stood for photographs, I could feel the heat through my double-breasted waistcoat, and beneath my top hat.

We took the short but bumpy ride up to Whaley Bridge Cricket Club, and as we pulled into the gate, the unmistakeable sound of helicopter rotors could be heard overhead. The first one came into view, and then the other. They landed on the immaculately mowed outfield, and then we waited for the rotors to completely stop. The smaller of the two was almost entirely black, whilst the larger machine had emerald green livery on its black exterior. Its registration, that began ONTV, was because it was one of the helicopters that had been used on *Anneka Rice's Treasure Hunt*.

We split into two groups, with Sally accompanying the boys in the smaller helicopter, based very roughly on weight, whilst myself, Fiona and Gabi went into the larger beast. There were more photos and videos, and even at that early stage the girls were concerned about their phone batteries. There was a brief safety demonstration, and we were away. Our pilot took the lead, given that he was easily the more experienced of the two, and within minutes, we had cleared the two reservoirs of Fernilee and Errwood. He was ultra-professional, and I thought it best not to tell him that when we returned there would actually be a cricket match in progress on the cricket pitch.

Our average flying altitude was around twelve hundred feet, and so everything on the ground was crystal clear. However, with nothing else to do I found myself looking down for far too much of the journey, resulting in quite a stiff neck. We crossed over Alton Towers, and then headed for the M40. Bicester, Oxford and Henley-On-Thames could all be clearly seen from the air, and our pilot gave us the lowdown on things that he had to avoid, such as microlight aircraft, gliders and parachutists.

After around seventy-five minutes, Ascot came into view, and we flew over the home straight which proved to be another great photo opportunity. We swung around and landed in a large field, from where we were accompanied to the reception area by the ground staff. Our pilots would park up and be taken to the golf course to be fed and watered for the day, ensuring that they would be fresh for our return journey later.

The reception area was a rather grand marquee, with a check-in desk at one end, where they issued us a card with the details for our return flight, and a bar at the other end. The complimentary champagne flowed rather freely, whilst I opted for a grapefruit juice followed by a bottle of Peroni. Zac took the opportunity to open his study book as he had an A Level exam the following day, but I think that was the last time his book saw the light of day.

Pastries were offered, and there was a supply of Royal Ascot racecards. I picked one up. It was different to any other racecard, with a decidedly antique feel inferring its quality and value. It was a proud moment to see Star Of Lady M listed in the sixth race. I was anxious to get to the course, collect our badges and go inside so that we could relax, but the girls wanted more of the complimentary champagne. My nerves ratchetted up another notch. Eventually, we boarded a Mercedes people carrier and set off to cover the short distance to the course. The driver followed the signs to Car Park 8, but I knew that our badges were at Car Park 2. This was more stress that I could do without, but worse was to come. The roads were already getting busy with raceday traffic, and I was thankful that we were not paying the standard £45 to park our car in a field. We reached Car Park 8, and the driver described the pick-up situation by stating that there would be cars about marked with the heliport insignia. We would just have to locate one and then all would be taken care of. I was not convinced, and then I insisted that he took us to Car Park 2.

We soon discovered that Car Park 2 was on the other side of the course and walking there in that heat would have been a disaster. As it turned out, it might have been quicker, as we got stuck in traffic on Ascot high street. My nerves were starting to shred, with still around five hours until race time, and then we discovered at least part of the cause for the delay. The Royal family were heading in the opposite direction, in preparation for the Royal procession. So, we waited, inched forward, stopped, and waited some more. Around forty-five minutes later, we passed the entrance to Car Park 2. The instructions said that the Owners & Trainers facility was at the west end of Car Park 2, but the signs simply stated L and R. We gambled, and it paid off, as we walked in right by the aforementioned facility. Five minutes later, we had our individually named Owners badges, as well as parade ring passes for race 6.

The entrance was on the other side of a busy road, and after being herded across by an efficient steward, we underwent a thorough bag check before stepping across the threshold onto the hallowed grounds of Royal Ascot.

The signs inside were about as good as those outside. We wandered aimlessly for a while, taking in the grandeur of the grandstand, the bustling throngs, and the decorated Queen Anne Enclosure. The Royal Enclosure had its own rules, though some of these only extended until after the Royal procession, which seemed rather odd. I found an information desk to ask for directions to the Owners bar, and a surprised lady said that she did not think that there was one. She then unfolded a map from the centre of one of the racecards, and she pointed us to the Bustino and Grundy lawn area that we had just walked past.

It was now approaching 1pm so we settled ourselves at an Owners bar with a jug of Pimm's and more Peroni. The temperature must have been approaching thirty degrees out on the manicured lawns, where every table had already been reserved. I would not normally eat before Star Of Lady M had raced due to frayed nerves, but in this case, with still four and a half hours to go, we all agreed that we should dine as soon as possible. Fiona went in search of a restaurant, and she came back a short time later having achieved her goal. We followed her lead and meandered through corridors and another bar before finally arriving at a crowded restaurant. We were seated at the far end, and, quite bizarrely, our table was number 22, the same number as Star Of Lady M in the Windsor Castle. It was an omen. I laughingly suggested that we would finish twenty-second, but that was quickly dismissed. The buffet style lunch was excellent, and after several cold meats with rice, pasta and various other side dishes, I attacked the chocolate pudding, strawberries and clotted cream with gusto. Two glasses of wine washed it all down, and then we once again braved the heat outside.

We took up our position in the Owners viewing area to watch the Royal procession. The Prince of Wales and the Duchess of Cornwall, otherwise known as Charles and Camilla, took the lead as the carriages made their way down the course. This kind of spectacle is what makes Royal Ascot so special to so many people, but to be honest, I just wanted to get on with the racing.

We met Luke Lillingston and his wife, Tabitha, and they were as excited as we were at the prospect of Star Of Lady M running at Royal Ascot. I had failed to get Tabitha an additional parade ring pass, but Luke had worked his magic so all was well. We went our separate ways, aiming to meet up in time for our race, and then we settled in for the rest of the racing. Temperatures continued to soar, and I opted for water to stave off dehydration. The first race was the Queen Mary, and of course, on a different day that might have been our chosen contest. As it turned out, our regular jockey, Danny Tudhope, rode the winner and I had backed him. Zac had bet £10 each way rather than £5 by mistake, and so his betting reserves were already seriously depleted. Gabi had never been to a race meeting before, and she quickly burnt through her funds as well. I backed the third winner at good odds, and then we decided to try to find somewhere out of the stifling heat. The bar was now full, making it even hotter than before, and eventually we settled for a table with two chairs at one end of the lawn just away from the pre-parade ring. A waitress took our order, and I opted for a vodka as well as my usual water, just to calm my nerves. A combination of heat and nerves is not good, and I was starting to suffer. It was around 4.45pm, and the Royal Hunt Cup was just fifteen minutes away. I went for a walk and noticed some of the horses for the Windsor Castle coming into the pre-parade ring. My nerves climbed to another level, and I went to sit back down. My hat was off, my jacket was off, and now I unbuttoned my waistcoat. This felt like being released from a straitjacket, but as time ticked on, I was honestly not sure whether I would be able to make the race, and particularly the preliminaries.

My phone buzzed. It was Luke beckoning us to the pre-parade. I galvanised myself and, accompanied by concerned and excited family, we went to meet him. Star Of Lady M was nowhere to be seen; they were clearly keeping her out of the heat. I met Jason Kelly and Char-lee Heard, and they were busy but relaxed. We found Luke and Tabitha, and we also met John O'Kelly who was the auctioneer when we bought Star Of Lady M. I suggested that he might have brought the hammer down just a little quicker, and that raised a smile. I was over the effects of the heat, but my nerves were dreadful.

Star Of Lady M finally emerged from her stable and went straight to the parade ring. She looked magnificent, and her appearance was made even more special by the Royal Ascot saddle cloth with gold numbers and lettering. As we made our way there, other runners were already heading out onto the course. We were very late, but I think this was a deliberate ploy to keep her away from the hullabaloo for as long as possible. The pre-parade ring had been busy, but the parade ring was far worse. It was impossible to see anyone. Luke spotted our trainer, David O'Meara, and we followed Jason through to a small gap where David was giving last minute instructions to our jockey, Colin Keane. Sally appeared a short time later, just in time to see David give Colin a leg up. They both looked relaxed, and we made our way to the packed grandstand with reserved optimism. Gabi grabbed me another water along the way, and as we peered towards the start, Star Of Lady M walked calmly into stall 1, the first horse to be loaded. Her odds had stabilised at 33/1, unlike my stomach which was churning as I waited for the other twenty-three to go in.

After what seemed like an eternity, they were off. Star Of Lady M got out better than she had in any of her previous four starts, then Little Big Bear was driven to pass her. It was going well until the field tacked across to the centre. Colin Keane tried to straighten her but she fought against him. She changed her legs and then seemed to get bumped. It was clear that she was not going to win, so Colin eased her through the second half of the race with hands and heels. There was no reason to give her a hard race, particularly in the burning heat, and she trailed in towards the back. Little Big Bear won the race, and Star Of Lady M was, well, we might have guessed, twenty-second.

Chapter Twenty-Seven

My nerves had disappeared completely and a swathe of relief washed over me as we realised that her race was run. We rushed down to the unsaddling area, where Colin had already dismounted. I wondered if she had sustained an injury, maybe sore shins, but Colin was fine with her. He said that she is uncomplicated with good speed, but the ground was plenty fast enough for her. David confirmed that there was nothing wrong with her, and we stood debating the outcome for quite some time. We all agreed that with a middle draw it could have been different, but that's racing. It was not our day, but everyone was convinced that she would bounce back. Our next target would be a Listed race to try to get black type, which would increase her value as a broodmare. The options were either the Dragon Stakes at Sandown, or Deauville in France which was a more likely destination. David had to go off to saddle a runner in the last race, and he said that he would be in touch in the next few days.

Tabitha introduced us to her mum, and Sally immediately spotted that her name badge read "Lady Ross", but she preferred Susie. The conversation inevitably turned to horses, and in particular an occasion earlier in the year. Sally had picked up Luke and Tabitha's daughter, Lara, from Bakewell after her Duke of Edinburgh event, and she reported back that as soon as she saw that Sally's car was full of bridles, saddles and other tack she knew that she was alright, and Susie concurred. Susie owned a piece of Mehmar who had finished a few places in front of us in the Windsor Castle. It was probably the most relaxed twenty minutes of the whole day, but we had to move on so we said our goodbyes.

We somehow ended up in the Royal Enclosure for the final race of the day, but I was certainly not bothered about having another bet. Once the racing was done, I had made a profit, while Gabi and

Zac had not had a single winner. The most memorable result came when Ole's horse beat Sally's in a photo finish. Fiona continued her obsession with Danny Tudhope by backing his winner in the first. However, it was the majesty of Royal Ascot that left the biggest impression.

We were fortunate to find a steward who pointed us in exactly the right direction for the helicopter pick-up. We had to walk down the course, around a marquee, and then across the track. Our original driver just happened to be waiting for us on the other side. Less than ten minutes later, we were back at the helicopter reception, with the girls making the most of the champagne that was still on offer. I had more water and grapefruit juice, and just before 7pm our pilots were ready to take us back to Whaley Bridge.

Our route replicated the outward journey, including another bird's eye view of Alton Towers. As we approached our destination, I messaged the club to ensure that the pitch was clear for our arrival. It took us around seventy-five minutes again, and as we touched down the assembled crowd took photos and videos from their elevated positions along the banking at Whaley Bridge Cricket Club. I decided we should look our best, so I donned my top hat and tails again and stepped out to a round of applause.

Some friends had arranged a champagne reception for our arrival, but I settled for an ice cold Vimto. We returned home, and as is tradition I headed for the Drum & Monkey. I was exhausted, but felt that I had to make the trip. I was joined by Fiona, as well as her son, Jake, and his fiancée, Aimee. One pint later, we headed back home where Gabi, Sally and the boys were tucking in to a takeaway. I had a few chips but could not face any more.

It had been a marvellous day, and the helicopters certainly surprised the village. Even in 2022, when someone hears those thudding rotors, they always look up, point, and shout, "Helicopter". I am not sure I would like to travel much further in a helicopter, seventy-five minutes was just about my limit. The blistering heat was also something that I needed to manage better, as were my nerves. One thing is for certain though, for the six of us that made the trip, our day at Royal Ascot was one that we would never forget.

After a good night's sleep, I watched the race back, and everything that we had discussed immediately afterwards was reiterated. She had not had a hard race, but the journey and the heat would have taken plenty out of her. Perhaps she would be ready in time for the Dragon at Sandown which was just fifteen days away, or perhaps it would be better to wait for Deauville on 10th July, regardless. In my mind, I had decided on Deauville, which also meant that the next countdown could begin. We were twenty-four days away from her next race.

Chapter Twenty-Eight

We had an anxious wait until the message came through from Gina that Star Of Lady M had returned safe and sound, and none the worse for her experience. I spoke to Richard Kent and he was fully in support of heading for a Listed event in France. He had a filly that had unfortunately finished fourth when he tried it the previous year.

Her ratings were understandably low. A TopSpeed of 18 and an RPR of 45 were only to be expected, but I also noticed that there had been some adjustments to previous RPRs. These were now 74, 76, 68, and 87, with TopSpeeds of 51, 80, 40 and 66. It was a little bewildering, but I thought no more of it and got around to social media. I thanked everyone for their help and support, and I was touched by the responses that were unanimous. Everyone was so pleased that Star Of Lady M had made it to Royal Ascot, even though most of them had lost money on her on this particular occasion. They wanted to know that she was safe and well, and they looked forward to her next outing.

I made special mention of David O'Meara and his team who managed the whole process of travel and pre and post-race activities so well, and also of Colin Keane who gave her the best possible race in the circumstances. I would certainly love to have him on board again whenever Danny Tudhope was unavailable. Finally, without Luke and Tabitha, we would not have had the same experience. Tabitha was such a calming voice amid the chaos, whilst Luke pushed on and cleared any obstacles in our way. As ever, his post-race assessment was spot on, and I looked forward to my next conversation with him.

I decided to check my Weatherbys bank account to see what our day at Ascot had cost from a racing perspective, and I made some interesting discoveries. Our jockey, Colin Keane, did not have VAT attached to his fee, and our share of the sponsorship, for having a saddle cloth embellished with both Royal Ascot and Longines insignia, was just £20.24. We did not even get any appearance money as we had at Chester. However, much more interesting than this were the additional payments. There was a £10 debit for the Foreign Racing Handling Charge, and there was a debit of £18.59 for Star Of Lady M to be registered with France-Galop, the administrators of racing in France. These had actually been processed a month or so earlier. It must have taken that amount of time to complete the process, but it was certainly auspicious less than twenty-four hours after the Ascot race.

So, we were definitely off to France, or so it seemed. The next few hours were spent researching trains, planes and automobiles to get to Deauville for a Sunday afternoon meeting. Flying to Paris would be the obvious one, but with the chaos at most airports at the time this would be so stressful. It was also probably three and a half hours from Paris airport to Deauville, making the door-to-door time somewhere close to ten hours. Driving would be quicker, but then there were rules about cars and adaptations that would need to be made. In addition, although the journey time could be under nine hours, it could also end up being closer to twenty hours given the UK roads.

A ferry from Portsmouth would take us close to Deauville, but the crossing could take eight hours or so, and then there was Eurostar. My sister is a seasoned traveller, and she said that she would not consider any other way. Business class to Paris Gare Du Nord was the way to go, and that would include free food and drink as well as lounge access at both ends. That more or less settled it, travelling Saturday morning and returning Sunday evening.

Unfortunately, Sally was unavailable that weekend, so I asked my nephew Jake, and Neil Woolley, both of whom owned a share in Emerald Duchess. Neil was a definite almost immediately, and Jake would be except for one small problem, he did not have a passport. He had applied for a new one two weeks ago, but the wait time could be up to ten weeks. I booked a hotel for myself and Neil, but I ensured that it was one that could be extended to three people if necessary. The trains would have to wait until we were definitely going as they were non-refundable.

Our nearest major train station is Macclesfield, and on Sunday evenings, the last train back from London Euston to there is 9.30. That would be a close shave to connect from the Eurostar, so I looked at Derby which is about an hour away. That was a much better connection, with the added advantage that the train from Derby goes directly into St Pancras where the Eurostar departs from. So that was decided. We would go from Derby to St Pancras, then Eurostar to Paris, followed by an onward train to Deauville. With twenty-three days left until the race, it was all sorted.

Luke called and said that he had decided to give us a day to recover and relax before he contacted us. Once again, he was as excited to learn about the next part of our adventure as we were. He confirmed that racing in France is a lot more relaxed than in England, and he knew plenty of people in Deauville. However, he was not exactly sure what the arrangements were for Owners. I did some research and emailed France-Galop. They responded quite quickly and said that when our horse was entered into a race in France, we would automatically have an account created. From that account, I would be able to apply for Owners badges.

As expected, Emerald Duchess was not declared to run at Pontefract as the forecast rain did not arrive, and Fittleton Ferry was pulled out of her race as she was having treatment on her back.

Chapter Twenty-Nine

The following weekend there was a deluge of biblical proportions in the forecast, so I emailed Tim to suggest that there were races at Pontefract, Thirsk and Haydock that we might consider. The Pontefract race was the Class 2 Spindrifter, and although we would be a little out of our depth in that contest, there were usually only four or five runners declared which would give her a very different racing experience, as well as a genuine chance of some prize money.

Tim emailed back to say that he considered Thirsk to be one of our options, but he also suggested that Carlisle on the Saturday might be a possibility. I was just pleased that we were close to another run for the Duchess, but there was the nightmare scenario that we might run at Sandown with Star Of Lady M on Friday, followed by heading the seven to eight hours north to Carlisle for Emerald Duchess the following day. For now, though, there was nothing to do but wait, and for the first time in a while, I could get through the next few days without expecting any horse updates.

The official ratings (OR) for two-year-olds were published, and Star Of Lady M was given a mark of 86. This seemed reasonable, although I was convinced that there was more to come from her. Two of her rivals were significantly below this, with Primrose Ridge on 83 and Absolutelyflawless on 82. We were a long way short of horses such as Maria Branwell on 100 and Walbank on 102.

With seventeen days to go to the Deauville race, Emerald Duchess was entered into the race at Thirsk. There were forty-four entries, and she had an elimination sequence of ten, so we would require either a lot of entries to not be declared or the race to divide for us to get in. There was still a lot of rain in the forecast, more so for Carlisle than Thirsk.

Two days later, I received a message from Jason Kelly. Star Of Lady M was entered into the Dragon Stakes at Sandown, but they were also looking at the Yacowlef in Deauville. They were conscious that she had been very busy up to Royal Ascot, and so would not be looking to race her against a field of horses that had perhaps just missed out at Royal Ascot. As it turned out, that is exactly what the initial entries for the Dragon looked like. Walbank was in there, as was Brave Nation and Rocket Rodney, all rated above 100. Eddie's Boy (96) and Bakeel (95) were also in the mix, but if none of those five were declared, we would have a chance. A very optimistic view.

Absolutelyflawless had skipped Royal Ascot for the Listed Empress Stakes at Newmarket. She ran disappointingly, which seemed to be an endorsement that Royal Ascot was not really worth missing.

Fittleton Ferry was entered into and then withdrawn from another race with what seemed like a bruised foot. She was certainly not proving to be an easy horse to train.

On Monday morning, the declarations were made for Thirsk. We declared, along with twenty-nine others, and with so many declarations the race divided into two. We were in the first division, drawn 1 of fifteen, the worst possible draw with a bias in favour of high numbers. We had 3lb claimer Sean Kirrane on board. Duran Fentiman had ridden her on her two previous runs, but he was on another Tim Easterby horse, Mister Sox. I think that we had Sean because the conditions of the race meant that we only received a 3lb allowance from some of the cheaper colts, as the weights were determined by purchase price. Sean would give us another 3lbs.

The race did not look to be of the highest quality, with Richard Fahey's Craven installed as the 4/1 favourite. Second best in the market was priced at 14/1 with everything else at either 20/1 or 50/1. We were at 50/1. The odds quickly changed, with the favourite at 6/4 and Emerald Duchess in to 33/1. The analysts were not optimistic, commenting that she had previously been slowly away and lots more was needed. There was still a possibility that we would be entered at Carlisle, which would give us an option should the ground remain Firm at Thirsk, but this was not necessary. So, it would be a drive up to Thirsk on Wednesday morning, the same day that the declarations for the Dragon Stakes were due.

Early Wednesday morning, the Dragon Stakes entries were ticking up very slowly. With fifteen minutes left there were only five, then one more was added. Jason could see what was and was not entered, and although Walbank and Brave Nation were not declared, three of the declarations were rated 102, 96 and 95. We agreed that finishing fourth in the Dragon was not really much good for us, and so she was scratched. At the same time, she was entered into the Yacowlef at Deauville.

Tim was at Thirsk and said that the main aim of today's run for Emerald Duchess was to get a handicap mark. Horses are given a handicap mark after three races, and this was her third outing. We met Sean Kirrane, our young jockey who was taking 3lbs off her back, and he was a confident pilot. He had ridden her many times at home, which was very reassuring.

Tim instructed Sean to give her a slap if she needed it, but otherwise to ride her hands and heels. We were still trying to win, but whatever happened we would get a handicap mark that would dictate much of her future racing career.

For the race itself, she got out better than previously, though there was still room for improvement. She quickened well when she was asked, and at one point she was in contention. She was outpaced in the middle third, but she could have still made up significant ground until she started hanging. Sean was reasonably pleased with her, though he did say that she still ran quite green. Her finishing position of tenth was perhaps less than she could have achieved with more experience, but it certainly hit the spot in terms of her likely handicap mark. Her RPR was 53, up from 47, whilst her TopSpeed was 2 which I found baffling. I thought that I should stop paying any attention to TopSpeed.

One of her issues during the race was that she hung to the right, and there was a suggestion afterwards that they might try a different bit, though at home she runs very straight. Tim was also not quite sure of her distance. He thought that perhaps seven furlongs on a left-handed track to counteract the hanging would be better for her. Chester would be an extreme example of this, but maybe somewhere like York, Redcar or Thirsk again would also do the trick.

There were many opportunities for that kind of race over the following few weeks. Her handicap mark would be announced on Tuesday, and if she came out of her Thirsk race well, we would see her on the racecourse within ten to fourteen days

Afterwards, Luke agreed with the assessment that she was green, and that she may benefit from further. She was outpaced early on but made good headway. She ducked to the right which the jockey tried to correct, and at that point she was treated very gently. Luke certainly thought she had a good deal of ability. It was still only June and she had already run three times. She was seven and a quarter lengths off the winner (which was closer than previous races), and she was five places in front of Tim's other horse that finished last.

The following day, Tim was pleased to report that she had come out of the race well, and although they did not yet know why she hung to the right, he assured us that they would sort it out. With the likelihood of her needing seven furlongs, she would probably be scratched from the two October races that were both over six. The next stage of those was due in less than a week.

Chapter Thirty

The Yacowlef entries closed on Friday 1st July, but it seemed that it would be Monday 4th before I would be able to see them. I scanned the other French two-year-old races and found that they generally had at least ten, and often many more entries. However, a Class 2 contest at Saint-Cloud over six and a half furlongs had nine entries, of which five were forfeited leaving just four runners. That would not leave much a of a spectacle, but as an owner it would be great.

Jason would be able to see the Yacowlef entries at the closing time on the Friday and that is when a decision would be made. He also stated his intention to keep Star Of Lady M in the October races.

I heard nothing from Jason, and as I was browsing through the France-Galop site, I searched for Star Of Lady M. I found her with her entry for the Yacowlef, and that then allowed me to see the rest of the entries. There were sixteen in total, and some very highly-rated individuals. Five had an RPR higher than our filly, including Malrescia from George Boughey's yard. Mark Johnston had entered Beautiful Eyes. Havana Angel had an entry, and she had been bought the previous day for 320,000 euros.

It was disappointing as it seemed to be a very strong race, and Jason agreed. We were tending towards not declaring, as it was a tough journey for a young horse, and with a big, high-class field it would not be worth the risk. We would keep an eye on the next stage, which was the following Wednesday, and if the race did cut up, we could still declare, but that would mean a lot of last-minute travel arrangements.

We discussed alternatives, and there were not many, particularly as David O'Meara wanted to keep her at five furlongs for now. Jason also said that they did not want to force her into a race, it would be better to wait for the right opportunity. As ever, he was absolutely correct. She had already raced five times, and a prolonged break would see her resume fresh for the opportunities in August, September, and October. I did a little more research, and I added the Group 3 Arenberg in Paris on 1st September as another potential engagement.

By Monday, two days before the next stage of the Yacowlef, I discovered that Havana Angel had been bought to race in the US, so perhaps she would not run. In addition, six of the other runners had alternative engagements, including the three top-rated entries. If they all took their alternative options rather than the Yacowlef, we would be the joint second highest-rated horse, just 3lbs below the favourite. Perhaps Deauville was still a viable option.

The following day, it all changed again. I got a call from Jason Kelly and we had a long and productive discussion regarding targets. He said that the Yacowlef could be a tough race on very firm ground and the journey was not something that should be undertaken lightly. The weekend could effectively derail the rest of her season. He also reiterated that David was not keen to send her there, and it would perhaps be different if she was in good form. However, on the back of Ascot he wanted to give her an easy time. The Ascot race itself would not have taken much out of her, but the travelling, heat, and the whole atmosphere might have affected her in ways that were perhaps not obvious. It would also cost around £6,000 just to get her to Deauville and back.

So, I cancelled the hotel and closed down the browser tabs with details of Eurostar and other transport methods. We were not going to Deauville, and with no set race in our sights I did not have to worry about my countdown. I could relax until such time as our next entry was made.

Chapter Thirty-One

David does not like his horses to stop and start. Instead, he puts them on lighter work and steps it up again when an entry is found. Jason thought that we should target the St Hugh's at Newbury on 12th August, a fillies-only Listed race that was also on my list. It could fall at just the right time, but the Julia Graves Roses at York eight days later was also a possibility.

It meant that I could relax for a few weeks, although we also talked about a prep race before the St Hugh's. This could either be a six-furlong nursery at Newmarket, or the Alice Keppel at Glorious Goodwood. The Newmarket race would give us an opportunity to see whether she stayed six furlongs, and Newmarket was generally seen as an easy six as it is downhill. The two October races that we had stayed in were both over six, so we needed to find out if they were a genuine option. The Alice Keppel was a Class 2 five-furlong race, and in the past two renewals there have only been seven runners each time. Newmarket is second only to York in terms of having a runner, and I have always considered Glorious Goodwood to be a laid-back version of Royal Ascot, so either would have been a good option.

It was always good to talk to Jason, he is clear and gives a good explanation for the decisions that we should make. I am perhaps spoilt by his approach which encourages a conversation or at least a message every ten days or so.

By contrast, Tim Easterby is a man of few "online" words, although face-to-face, he is very amiable and talkative. He calls when necessary, and he seems to want to ensure that whenever a conversation is required, he is the man to do it. Tim's updates often come at the racetrack, or even at the sales, which I quite like. There is nothing wrong with that, it is simply a different approach. The two trainers also have a different way of invoicing. Our monthly bills appear by email from David's yard, whereas Tim relies on the old-fashioned postal service.

On the latest bill from Tim, I noticed that we had been charged £190 for a vet to treat Emerald Duchess for a laceration above her right eye. This was news to us, although it had happened prior to Star Of Lady M going to Royal Ascot. It did not bother me particularly, but some in the syndicate wanted to know more. Perhaps Tim forgot, or perhaps he did not think that it was important enough to tell us. It was just his way, and for anyone thinking of entering the world of racehorse ownership, I would advise you to check out the communication style of your prospective trainer to ensure that it is one that suits you. You are, after all, investing a lot of money.

One of Tim's aims at the Thirsk race was to get Emerald Duchess a handicap rating. That came through as 54, which I thought was perhaps a couple of pounds too high. However, it should now pave the way for handicap entries, and we could look forward to her next run.

I met Edwina Currie for lunch, as she expressed an interest in taking up one of the three remaining shares in Emerald Duchess. She lives in our village, and I had become friendly with her through her business club. It was an interesting conversation, as she told me about her previous involvement in racing. This included the television series *Wife Swap* in which she swapped her husband for John McCririck. When I explained the opportunity with Emerald Duchess, she joined The 1891 Group syndicate without hesitation.

Chapter Thirty-Two

I probably should have moved on from the Yacowlef, but at the first forfeit stage I had a look to see who had pulled out. As expected, Havana Angel was gone, as was the 93 rated Lova. However, all of the other principals, including the two UK-trained horses, were still there. There were two more forfeit stages to go, as well as a supplementary option, but I was happy with our decision which was the best thing for Star Of Lady M.

Thursday came around and there were still nine runners in the Yacowlef, including the top-rated horse, Wootton Bay, and the English competitor, Malrescia. Most of the withdrawals had been lower rated, whilst there was one supplementary entry. At that point, we would have been the joint fourth highest on ratings.

Emerald Duchess was duly scratched from the two October 1st races, but there were still a lot of entries in each. The Redcar Two-Year-Old Trophy had reduced from 293 to 193, whilst the Tattersalls auction race at Newmarket had come down from 223 to 168. I had mentioned to Jason that the Newmarket race looked to be a bit of a lottery with thirty runners, whereas at Redcar the field was generally fifteen to twenty. He countered this as the Redcar race was Listed, and tended to attract a better quality of horse. The Newmarket contest ought to have been easier to get at least a place.

There was nothing more to think about. The earliest entry for Star Of Lady M to watch out for would not be for at least two weeks, and there were no seven-furlong races for Emerald Duchess for another week or more. So, I could relax and watch the Brocklesby winner Persian Force win comfortably at Newmarket.

I did wonder whether earlier entries might occur, but nothing came about. Then I looked at the Yacowlef result, which proved that we were right to bypass the contest, as the three top-rated horses filled the first three places.

Fittleton Ferry was entered at Ffos Las. It was an odd choice of event as it was not a handicap, which meant that she was worse off at the weights than in previous starts. It was over seven and a half furlongs, and not much was expected of her. Despite her speed, she struggled in the early part of the race, but she did manage to run on into ninth position of the fourteen runners. An RPR of 30 and a TopSpeed of 4 were entirely predictable, and I am not hopeful of any improvement in the near future.

I thought that I had a good handle on potential dates for Star Of Lady M and Emerald Duchess, so I dispensed with the BHA race search website for a couple of days. Then, somewhat out of left field, Star Of Lady M had an entry for a five-furlong handicap at Musselburgh the following Tuesday, two days before the Alice Keppel entries. I messaged Jason and he said that he was still looking at the Alice Keppel and the Newmarket six-furlong handicap, but the Musselburgh race was likely to cut up and that would be a better option. He thought that it would be more like a decent piece of work on grass rather than a race, and we would still have a reasonable chance of winning. We would certainly be in with a chance of some prize money. The winner of the race would earn just short of £6,700, so it was not the biggest prize, but perhaps I had been spoilt.

Chapter Thirty-Three

Jason's reasoning made sense as there were only nine entries, which meant that the final field could be just four or five runners. Teatime Tipple and Fragrance were both entered, but in my mind, the biggest danger was Jungle Time. We would have to give away a lot of weight all round, but it would give us that extra week to prepare for the St Hugh's at Newbury which was still our ultimate aim.

My internal countdown clock started ticking at six days, and my thoughts turned to Musselburgh. First of all, I had to confirm exactly where it is. Five miles east of Edinburgh, and whilst it was a four-and-a-half-hour drive, the train could potentially take even longer. The train would also be rather expensive, a somewhat ironic stance given that our last trip with Star Of Lady M was by helicopter. My mind was quickly made up. We would drive on the morning of the race, stay at one of the local castles, and drive back the following day. The biggest decision was, which castle? We would also have to hope that Emerald Duchess would not run at Lingfield the day after the Musselburgh race, a distinct possibility, but fortunately one that did not materialise.

The weights were announced the following day, and we had to give lots of weight to just about every other horse. These included Dickieburd who would be 5lbs lighter, Explicit, 9lbs lighter, and Fragrance, ten. Howaydaoin would carry a huge 26lbs less than us. Jason Watson was listed as our jockey. Jason was another of David O'Meara's stable jockeys, so we were confident that he would have ridden Star Of Lady M plenty of times at home. He would also be familiar with her pace, as he rode Primrose Ridge when Star Of Lady M won on debut.

As time wore on, several of the mounts had jockeys assigned. Dickieburd had always had a rider listed, but now the two Mark Johnston horses also had experienced riders on board. Teatime Tipple had a 5lb claimer.

On the Saturday before our race, and the day before our declarations, there was a three-year-old race at Newbury that originally had thirteen entries. When it came to declarations, there were none. Every horse had pulled out. Whilst that would be easy to pick up prize money, it would not be great if it happened in our race. It had been a while since Star Of Lady M raced and she needed some exercise.

The sad thing about the Newbury race was that it was a GBB race for fillies only. So, someone had thrown a massive pot away.

There was also some welcome news from Newbury when Massaat sired Hectic to win the first race, and then Havana Grey's son Eddie's Boy won the Super Sprint. The Massaat result was particularly pleasing, as it should be just about the right time for his offspring to come to hand.

By 8am the following day, there were just two declarations for the race at Musselburgh. By 9.45, there were still just two, and then in the closing minutes another two were added. So, there were four runners, and one was a bit of a surprise. Karl Burke's Jungle Time had raced the previous Thursday, so would only have five days between races. We would have to concede 11lbs to that runner.

At the bottom of the weights, we would have to give 16lbs to Cuban Rock, and the other entry was Explicit.

As ever, the *Sporting Life* listed the odds. Jungle Time was at 6/4, with Star Of Lady M at 15/8, Explicit at 100/30 and Cuban Rock at 11/1. A short time later we were in to 6/4 favourite, with Jungle Time at 7/4, Explicit at 3/1 and Cuban Rock at 12/1. William Hill priced up all of the first three in the betting at 2/1, but that is the nature of handicapping.

The *Sporting Life* considered that although this was not as competitive as the Windsor Castle, her initial handicap mark may be a little harsh. It is not the first time they have been negative about Star Of Lady M. Meanwhile, in Australia she was proving to be very popular. Their *Racing and Sports* publication headlined with "O'Meara's Lady To Star At Musselburgh."

Britain was struck by a heatwave, and five meetings were cancelled due to the extreme heat. Musselburgh survived, but we kept a close eye on the temperatures and the possibility of a last-minute cancellation. We were certainly grateful that Musselburgh's standard dress code was "wear what you feel comfortable in".

It was the day before the Musselburgh race and I received a brief message from Tim Easterby. Emerald Duchess was well and in good form, and they were looking for a nursery for her. I had suggested Chester on 31st July or Thirsk on 5th August. He also said that she would run in a hanging bit to try to encourage her to run a little straighter next time. There was a sense of optimism that Emerald Duchess might finally start to show us something.

Chapter Thirty-Four

The following morning, we set off for Scotland, and the heat was stifling even as early as 7am. We hit the M6 and headed north in very light traffic. By the time we reached Carlisle the air was noticeably cooler, so we continued over the Scottish border and stopped for a break. We checked the *Sporting Life* website and Musselburgh was definitely on, so we booked a room at Melville Castle, just a few miles from the racecourse. It was still another hour and a half away, so we called ahead and asked them to book a taxi to take us to the course.

Almost five hours after leaving home we pulled into the elegant surroundings of Melville Castle. We were greeted by suits of armour and huge tapestries, with pleasant gardens surrounded by mature trees and bushes. Check-in was quick as our room was ready, so we had a quick change and jumped into our waiting taxi. I had a call with Jason Kelly, and he was comfortable that she was only facing three rivals. He thought Jungle Time and Explicit would vie for the lead and we would track in behind. If the weight did not hold her back, she would then challenge late. I also asked him if this was the only race before the St Hugh's but he was non-committal. He thought that if she won at Musselburgh, or just ran a good race, then the St Hugh's would be next, but there may still be an opportunity to run her in the Alice Keppel at Goodwood. The entries for that were two days away, so it was becoming a hectic time of the season.

Musselburgh racecourse was about fifteen minutes away, and we were given Owners & Trainers badges, racecards, and lunch vouchers on our arrival. It was still early, and our race was not until 4.10pm, so we had an excellent ham salad for lunch in the Harris Tweed bistro, before heading into the Owners & Trainers marquee. The temperature was certainly bearable, especially when the clouds drifted across the sun, so we had beer and champagne and watched the early races. Sally seemed to have the golden touch, backing several winners, whereas I seemed to struggle with seconditis.

There is a viewing section in the stand reserved for Owners & Trainers, and it had a great position overlooking the winning post. However, it seemed that it was a bit of a free for all, with no one checking badges.

Temperatures began to rise around 3pm, which is about the same time as my nerves started to kick in. They were certainly not as bad as at Royal Ascot, but as soon as the preceding race was finished and the horses returned to their stables, I was on the lookout for Star Of Lady M. We crossed into the parade ring, and with only four runners it was easy to see the other owners, but who was with which horse? Sarah, from David's yard, appeared, and we chatted about the weather, our castle, and Star Of Lady M. The conversation briefly took my mind off the impending race, but the nerves soon returned. Our filly appeared shortly afterwards, and she looked fantastic. She was relaxed, inquisitive, and taking in her surroundings. Jason Watson came to greet us, and he confirmed the tactics that I had discussed with Jason Kelly earlier. They headed for the start, so Sally and myself left the parade ring to take up a suitable spot in the grandstand. On our way there we were stopped by a couple of chaps who wanted to know if our horse would win. All that I could confirm was that I had backed her, and that seemed enough for them. Her odds of 9/4 were reasonable, with Explicit at 5/2 and Jungle Time the 5/4 favourite.

As expected, the Owners & Trainers part of the grandstand had a lot of people in it. There were only four runners, but maybe forty spectators. It made for a good atmosphere as the horses started to walk into the stalls.

Despite the small field there was a bump between Explicit and Star Of Lady M at the start, but it did not seem to have much effect. Jason Watson steadied Star Of Lady M in behind Explicit who was vying for the lead with Jungle Time on the rail. The leaders were three lengths clear of Star Of Lady M in the early stages, with Cuban Rock struggling in the rear.

Past half way and Jason asked her to quicken. For a while it looked like she would not make it, but she gradually started gaining. Explicit took the lead from Jungle Time and Star Of Lady M ranged alongside. She looked at her rivals, put her head down and sprinted to the finish going away. It was a massive weight carrying performance that resulted in an easy length and a half victory. The Owners & Trainers grandstand erupted, and it was not just Sally and myself. Many of the punters were waving betting slips emblazoned with Star Of Lady M, and we were offered plenty of handshakes and pats on the back. She had won £6,696, but the prize money was incidental; it was another victory.

In the parade ring, we headed for the space reserved for the winner and waited for our Star. She still looked fresh as she was washed down, and she was always ready for a bit off fussing after her races. Photographs followed, and then Jason was interviewed about the race, his only mount of the day. He said that she was an easy ride, and she travelled strongly to take the win as she liked. We had a presentation of four beautifully engraved glasses and a bottle of Edinburgh gin, then we went into a private suite to enjoy a couple of glasses of champagne and reruns of the race. The way commentators call the race is always fascinating, and in this instance, it was finished off nicely with "Star Of Lady M is going to give weight and a beating to her rivals, the class act of the race wins."

Eventually we made our way back to the Owners & Trainers marquee. As ever, once the race was over, we could relax. Luke messaged his congratulations but then called almost immediately. He was so thrilled and wondered aloud if she was the only two-year-old across Europe to have won four races this year. She was certainly the winning-most daughter of Havana Grey who was fast becoming a legend at stud.

Over a refreshing shandy, I spoke to Jason Kelly who was very impressed. He also suggested that she had not had a hard race, it was more like a piece of work. This meant that she could still go to Goodwood the following week before the St Hugh's on 12th August.

We bumped into James Callow, owner of the disappointing Cuban Rock. He was very complimentary about our filly, and we chatted to him and his party until well after the final race. It was a scene that we were very much getting used to, making new friends all with a similar love of racing. As new owners, it seemed that everyone was interested in our story, and so happy for our success. Twitter had exploded more than ever, possibly because Musselburgh was the only UK meeting of the day. I had many new followers, all offering their congratulations. There were a few issues leaving the course as taxis were few and far between, but as we waited at the taxi rank more people came up to us and told us that they had won on our horse. She seemed to be popular wherever we went.

We eventually arrived back at the hotel where we had dinner and sat on the outdoor terrace, watching the world go by against the backdrop of the castle. It had been an exhausting day after a long drive and the tension of the race.

The following morning, we set off early for the drive home, and I noticed that we had been given a mystifying TopSpeed of 58. I wondered what the RPR would be, and more importantly what her revised OR would be after such a convincing performance. We received the welcome message from Gina at the yard that she was well after her race and she had trotted up sound.

I spoke to Richard Kent who again suggested that we might get offers for her to race in California, particularly after carrying so much weight, but I told him we were not selling at any price. I also suggested that he might want a special golden door at his stud farm if we eventually sent her there as a broodmare, but he thought that Luke might want her at his Mount Coote stud. That was a conversation for way into the future.

Chapter Thirty-Five

The BHA website is never far away, and I noticed that we already had an entry for the Alice Keppel. This five-furlong Class 2 race for fillies only is on the Wednesday of Glorious Goodwood, and in previous seasons, it had cut up to just six or seven runners. Entries would close the following day, and I would be scrutinising them in real time. There was one big problem with the Alice Keppel, it was again the sixth race on the card. I wondered how on earth my nerves would cope for that length of time.

I logged on just after 8am the following morning, and the Alice Keppel entries already stood at five. They quickly increased to ten and kept on going. With a few minutes to go they had reached twenty-one, which was considerably more than I was expecting. Conversely, the Group 3 Molecomb, on the same day, only had ten entries. I messaged Jason and we agreed that a Molecomb entry would give us an additional option. It was a short conversation, but an incredible feeling that Star Of Lady M was good enough to even be considered for a Group race. With the Queen Mary at Royal Ascot, it was more for the experience, but now we were considering that we might actually have a chance at that level.

As the entries closed, I looked at the fields. I thought that we might be sixth favourite for the Molecomb, where top three would be the objective for black type. The Alice Keppel, which we needed to win to justify entering, and to pick up another GBB, would have us as perhaps fourth favourite. In the ante-post betting for the Molecomb, we were listed as joint eighth favourite at 20/1, with Rocket Rodney, Walbank and Eddie's Boy heading the market. In the Alice Keppel, ten had other entries, so a lot would change before the declarations stage the following Monday. There was also the possibility that we could skip Goodwood altogether and go straight for the St Hugh's at Newbury.

Later that day, we received the updated RPR from the Musselburgh race. We had been given 91, whilst Explicit had dropped from 77 to 75. I also noticed that Danny Tudhope was now listed as our jockey in the Alice Keppel, whereas previously he had been assigned to ride the Clipper Logistics newcomer, Eternal Class. That was good news, and perhaps meant that Eternal Class would not run.

Another day dawned with another racing engagement, this time the Music Showcase event at York. On our way up there, we called in at David O'Meara's to see Star Of Lady M who demanded attention. We also received a head collar from Beverley racecourse engraved with *Hilary Needler Winner 2022* to add to our growing collection of prizes.

At Middlethorpe Hall, our driver, Terry, dropped us off at the course, and we settled in for a fabulous evening in the Parade Ring restaurant. David O'Meara's mum Dympna rang me, and we met her and David by the parade ring. We talked about the trip to Musselburgh and David told us that he thought it was a fantastic performance by Star Of Lady M. He had not yet looked at the Alice Keppel entries, but he reiterated that it could cut up to a handful of runners. In the betting ring, I was once again hit by seconditis, and worse was to come in the sixth race when Danny Tudhope's mount could only finish fourth, denying me the placepot.

After racing, Tim Easterby came over to talk to us with his wife, Sarah, and son, Thomas. Tim and Thomas were both impressed by Emerald Duchess's latest piece of work, and Tim confirmed that the handicaps at Chester and Thirsk that I had suggested were both good options. He favoured the Thirsk race as it was for fillies only.

By lunchtime on Saturday the entries up to and including the following Friday had closed, and fifteen of the twenty-one Alice Keppel entries had alternatives. These included Puffable that ran the previous Thursday, Minnetonka and Cuban Mistress that were due to run later that day, and Cruise that was declared to run at Windsor on Monday. Of course, all of that meant nothing, and we would have to wait for the declarations the following Monday.

There was some positive news on Saturday, as Mascapone ran on for third in a Listed race, giving Massaat his first piece of black type.

On the Monday morning, I was due to have a scan on my knee at 9.20am, just forty minutes before the declarations closed. This would be an agonising wait, and I would have to catch up with Jason Kelly after my scan. It would give me little or no time to assess the situation, but I knew that Jason would have it covered.

Before I went in for the scan, the highly-rated colts had all been declared for the Molecomb, and so we agreed to scratch from that race.

At 9.37, Jason thought there might be some brinksmanship going on between ourselves, The Platinum Queen and Miami Girl, each waiting to see which of the others would declare. So, he decided to declare her and that was that.

By the time I emerged from the clinic the declarations were closed, and we were one of ten entries. Miami Girl had scratched, but The Platinum Queen was still there. Jason's view was that you should never be afraid of one horse, and our form was much stronger than most of the other runners. Jason mapped out the next few weeks, with the Alice Keppel being followed by the St Hugh's at Newbury. Next up would be a Listed race over six furlongs as preparation for whichever of the early closing races we opted for on 1st October.

Later that morning, I also found that Emerald Duchess had been entered into the handicap at Chester the following Sunday, along with eighteen other runners. There were a few previous winners in the field, but nothing too spectacular as you would expect in a handicap for horses rated less than 70. I knew that Thirsk was also a possibility, so I put the Chester entry to the back of my mind.

When the Alice Keppel was priced up, we were generally at 4/1 with 5/1 available in places. The Platinum Queen was the favourite at 6/4. Beautiful Eyes, who would have been favourite for the Lily Agnes, was in the race, as was Union Court. This filly had finished ninth in the Windsor Castle, at a shorter price than Star Of Lady M, and had run a creditable fifth in the Super Sprint. It was only our weight carrying victory at Musselburgh that had us favoured in the betting over that one. Richard Hannon, who had scratched Miami Girl, was represented by Cruise who was a non-runner for her Windsor race. Finally, All The Time, who had won first time out but finished last in the Queen Mary, was the only other fancied runner. It was interesting that she was as short as 12/1 for the Queen Mary, so they must have thought that she had ability. The other four were at very big prices. Just as at Royal Ascot, we were drawn in stall 1, and although with only ten runners this was not a huge problem, it was still a disadvantage compared with the favourite who was drawn in 8.

Chapter Thirty-Six

Luke Lillingston was featured in an article in the *Thoroughbred Daily News* (TDN), in which his success at the sales was highlighted. His quote about our journey was certainly memorable.

"She has given me huge pleasure as an agent this season. The Maddens asked me to buy them their first racehorse last year and we focussed on Book 3 because it suited our budget. She only cost 15,000gns and is eligible for the British bonuses. Including bonuses, she's earned the best part of £70,000. We bought another filly at that sale and she's with Tim Easterby. Her name is Emerald Duchess (GB) and she is by Massaat (Ire). She should be fun for them. The Maddens are bringing new people into racing and any time new people come into this sport, we should be very happy."

It was a reminder that bargains can be had, and we certainly had one.

The *Sporting Life* assessment of her chances for the Alice Keppel was a little more optimistic than normal, having Star Of Lady M as their second choice behind The Platinum Queen. They considered that she would be able to play a part in the race.

The day before the race, her new OR of 92 was announced, a rise of six which was fully justified based on her Musselburgh effort. Oddly enough, her RPR of 91 from that race was reduced to 89, but I was not going to dwell on that.

Our odds remained constant despite the favourite shortening to odds-on, with everything else drifting. I placed a bet to win, and we set off on our long journey down south. As we progressed south of Leicester on the surprisingly quiet M1, we passed a red horse wagon emblazoned with *David O'Meara Racing*. It was Star Of Lady

M, sensibly heading for the course a full twenty-four hours in advance. We reached our Airbnb in Easebourne by late afternoon, and with our limousine for the following day already booked, we went to the nearby town of Midhurst for a relaxing, alfresco dinner.

I had requested additional badges for Emerald Duchess's potential race at Chester, and then received a somewhat confusing message from a lady who would look into it once the Bangor declarations were confirmed the following day. It turned out she did the Bangor arrangements as well as Chester, and the automated PASS system form does not stipulate which racecourse the enquiry is for. Perhaps they need some better IT.

I messaged Simon Chappell, as I knew he would be at Goodwood, inviting him and his wife, Louise, to join us for the race. He was delighted and accepted immediately, and although I genuinely wanted them to be there for the fun of it, there was the underlying thought that they might just be able to distract me enough to quell the nerves.

The following morning, we were up bright and early and had a long soak in the hot tub that was in the garden of the Airbnb. Our host, Linda, was very interested in Star Of Lady M, and confessed that she had placed a small bet already. Her odds were drifting, and it seemed that all of the money was for The Platinum Queen. Most of our opponents were now 10/1 or more, whilst we were hovering around 11/2.

Goodwood is the centrepiece of a very British summer, and new outfits had to be procured. Sally opted for a very striking green, whilst I managed to find a colourful striped blazer, paired with pink shirt and trousers. I decided against the traditional Panama hat, I would save that for next year. Of course, the freedom of choice was so much more refreshing than the formal and regimented Royal Ascot.

We had a long wait for our limousine, but I received a message from Simon Chappell that his trainer, Scott Dixon, was holding a pre-race party in the Owners & Trainers car park, and would we like to join them? Of course we would. Finally, it was time to go, and our driver picked us up in a plush Jaguar for the short fifteen-minute journey to the course. Unlike Ascot, it was entirely possible to drive right up to the front entrance of Goodwood.

The Owners & Trainers car park was at the bottom of a small slope, and we soon found Simon and Louise, together with Scott Dixon, Matt Eves, and their partners, Becky and Sarah. Pimm's was immediately poured, and it all seemed very laid-back and relaxed. I could not help comparing it to our journey to Ascot when we were stuck in traffic on the high street for what seemed like an age, whilst all of the time my anxiety increased. Our very British version of a tailgate party had the opposite effect. Of course, the talk was all about horses, and Star Of Lady M got more than a few mentions. It was a welcome distraction, but we eventually made our way to the entrance to collect our badges. Perhaps it was the much lower temperatures, perhaps it was the meeting with friends beforehand, or perhaps it was just the laid-back vibe of Goodwood, but I was definitely not as nervous as at Royal Ascot.

Chapter Thirty-Seven

Within minutes we were inside, with time and space to look around. Everything was very well signposted, including the Owners & Trainers pavilion as well as the reserved viewing area. The view across the course to the South Downs was stunning, and so much nicer than the tented village and car parks of Ascot. We were already loving it, and just after 1pm we went to the Owners restaurant for a delicious buffet lunch. We mainly stuck to water, though I did manage a bottle of beer.

The build up to racing was in full swing, and when it began, I backed the first winner. It was a good start, and with three hours to go before our race, I was relatively calm. We wandered into the Owners pavilion, ordered a jug of Pimm's, and stood by the window admiring the sights and sounds of Glorious Goodwood. During lunch, we had spotted Tim Easterby, and he now came across to chat to us. He had arrived by plane, apparently a much more comfortable journey than by helicopter. He had not yet looked at the Chester entries, but he was happy to talk about all manner of things, including horses, of course, cricket, and children. We had just received a message that Ole and Zac had somehow managed to lock themselves out of the house, a distraction that I could well do without.

The second race passed us by as we were engrossed in our conversation with Tim, but I would have lost anyway so I'll take that as a winner. Tim wandered off just as the runners paraded for the next race. This was the Molecomb, the Group 3 that we had declined in favour of the Alice Keppel. I was very interested in the outcome, as there would always be thoughts of *could we have done better?* I did not back the winner, Trillium, which was a very fast Richard Hannon horse. It broke the course record, defeating the hot favourite, Rocket Rodney. Would that be an omen for the favourite in our race?

Tim came back and by then we had secured a table, so he sat down for more discussion. This time, we moved on to more serious matters, such as prize money and the Newbury race that was effectively boycotted. I pointed out that this was actually a fillies-only GBB race, and so £20,000 was on offer on top of the prize money, and Tim agreed. If they really want to get noticed, they should boycott a Listed or Group race, but that was very unlikely to happen. We also spoke about trainer communication, and he was very open to any ideas about improving this aspect. I have some ideas that could automate a lot of this, using the BHA website as a conduit. Trainers have to be on this website every day processing entries and declarations, and it could easily be extended to include one liners or more detailed updates on individual horses.

It was time for the superstar, Baeed, who duly won with a minimum of fuss, and I would have backed the second each way if I could have torn myself away from Tim. It was a fabulous hour or so, and with his all round knowledge it is easy to see why Tim is one of the top trainers.

I messaged Jason Kelly, and he replied that he was on his way, and he would see us at the course. That was encouraging as I did not know how chaotic the pre-race preparations would get, though they could not be as mad as at Royal Ascot.

Tim left to assist with Myristica, his horse in the 4.10. We wandered past the traditional huge strawberry tower, and the even bigger queues to partake of the tower, and took our place in the grandstand. We cheered Myristica on, but she could only finish a gallant fifth. It was now time for our race, so we sought out the pre-parade ring.

Across the manicured lawns and beyond the neat and tidy hedges, we spotted Star Of Lady M walking around with her groom. We went through the barriers and got as close as we dared, as she was taken back into her stable to be saddled. Jason Kelly emerged, followed by our filly, and she looked a picture. She walked calmly around, showing her usual level of interest. Jason had the opinion that the favourite was strong but we had a good chance. It was time to move to the parade ring, where we were joined by Simon and Louise Chappell, as well as Matt Eves. Chris Dixon, from RacingTV, a regular at David O'Meara's yard, also came over to us. They were all very complimentary about Star Of Lady M, even speculating what a good breeding programme might look like for her, but that was a few years away.

Danny Tudhope was back on board, and his only issue was with the draw. For the second, consecutive big meeting, we were unfavourably drawn in 1, but he had a plan to try to tuck in and track the leaders before delivering his challenge late. The bookmakers had us as joint second favourite with Union Court at 11/2, with The Platinum Queen firming up to odds-on.

Simon and Louise accompanied us into the stands, and with the constant chatter from the pre-parade ring all the way through the preliminaries, I had not had time to think about nerves. Could distraction be the key to overcoming this problem? Now they were starting to kick in, but before I had time to think about it, the race was off.

Danny's plan began well. He got out smartly and tucked in, tacking across towards the rail where The Platinum Queen was blazing a trail. The move cost a few lengths, but it kept us in the race. At half way, the favourite was still tearing up the course, and several in behind were struggling. We moved up to challenge, but the favourite kicked again. Ourselves and Union Court were the only realistic challengers, but The Platinum Queen surged clear to win by four lengths, breaking the new track record in the process. Danny eased Star Of Lady M down to finish third, a further two lengths behind the second placed, Union Court.

It was no disgrace to finish third to a horse that broke the track record and is almost certainly bound for Group success. She had even beaten the time set in the Molecomb. Star Of Lady M had done us proud, beating several fancied horses and previous winners. We had to pinch ourselves to believe that we had achieved a place at the second biggest meeting of the summer, and I was fairly sure that she had run faster than she ever had before.

Simon and Louise were delighted for us. Danny suggested that she might benefit from six furlongs, and that was certainly on the cards. However, for now, her excellent run confirmed that the St Hugh's at Newbury would be her next target. Jason was impressed, and for him it was "black type" all the way. The prize money was just over £6,000 but that was very much an incidental part of the day.

Without the victory, social media was not quite as explosive as on previous occasions, but there were plenty of goodwill messages. Of course, Luke was the first, and needless to say, he was very impressed.

We said our goodbyes and headed to the car park where our limousine was just a few minutes away. We got dropped off at the pub for pizza where a lot of the locals admitted to betting on our horse. Exhausted, we finally walked up the hill to our Airbnb.

As we reflected on the day, I could not help but compare our experiences at Royal Ascot and Goodwood. The former has pomp and circumstance, but Goodwood has the much more laid-back vibe. The drive to and from the course, the dress code, the entry process, the arrangements for Owners, the views across the course, and even the signposts made for a much more relaxing experience. The biggest difference was probably in the pre-parade and parade rings, where we actually had time to breathe, chat, and take in our surroundings. Of course, the heat at Royal Ascot did not help, but given the choice, I would return to Goodwood in a heartbeat. It truly was Glorious.

Chapter Thirty-Eight

The following morning, we had a soak in the hot tub before packing up our luggage and setting off on the long journey home. As we pulled over for a break, I checked the BHA website, and our entry for the St Hugh's was confirmed. We also received the always welcome note from Gina that Star Of Lady M was fit and well and had trotted out sound. So, fifteen days until her next race, the countdown could begin again.

We arrived home to a complimentary bottle of champagne and a free £50 bet courtesy of Tote World Pool, just for entering our horse at Goodwood. She received an RPR of 76, compared with The Platinum Queen's 105 and Union Court's 84. This was perhaps a little on the low side, but now that she had an OR it did not matter too much. Her TopSpeed of 75 was encouragingly high, but again, it had no effect on anything.

I assessed the Chester race that Emerald Duchess was entered into in three days' time. There was a total of nineteen runners, and none of them jumped out, as you would expect from a 0-70 nursery. I sent my thoughts to Tim, and the following day, he called just before the declarations were due to close. At that stage there were just six declared. He could see no reason not to enter her, and I agreed, so we could prepare for the short trip to Chester for their Sunday meeting. There were nine declared in total, but these included two that were due to run later that evening at Southwell. I messaged Richard Kent, and he told me that Evolicatt, another Massaat filly, was expected to win at Southwell, and would not be going to Chester. So, I backed her and waited for news. She duly won, with Breath Catcher some way adrift, and as expected, both horses were withdrawn from our race by Sunday morning. Not only did this mean that there were less opponents, it also meant that Emerald Duchess was guaranteed at least £500 prize money.

The *Sporting Life* were quite complimentary about Emerald Duchess, considering that she could improve over a longer trip, as she had shown some ability previously. However, the *Racing Post*'s Progeny app were not as enthusiastic. They thought that even her low mark was not enough based on her past performances.

Emerald Duchess opened at 16/1, and she quickly came in to 10/1. By the time Sunday came around she had drifted again, and was easily available at 16/1 and bigger. She looked well in the pre-parade ring, though perhaps just a little on her toes. In the parade ring, she had two handlers but there was still no cause for concern. Duran Fentiman was the jockey, and he confirmed that if she was in the firing line with a furlong to go, he would be throwing the kitchen sink at it. Her draw position of 6 was not ideal, but with only seven runners she was effectively in 5. We made our way to the viewing area on the top of one of the bars and waited for the action to unfold.

She had a problem with the break in previous races, and this time, although she got out quickly enough, she seemed to pause before joining the race. Within a few yards she moved from sixth to fifth, then dropped back to sixth and seventh. She made some headway passing a tiring outsider, but finished a disappointing sixth. The only horse to break worse than Emerald Duchess had actually run on strongly to finish a very close second, carrying 17lbs more than our filly. Duran thought that she might have needed the run after more than a month off. He said that she perhaps did not like the track, and he suggested that dropping back to six furlongs might help her. The ground was the opposite of what she was used to, being officially Good to Soft, Soft in places.

Luke and Richard were both disappointed, with Luke insisting that she must be better than that, whilst the normally optimistic Richard suggested that she did not seem to have learnt anything. It was a glum table back in the Owners & Trainers pavilion, but not for long. We were quickly back in good spirits thanks to Chester's excellent hospitality.

Emerald Duchess also had an entry for Thirsk on the Friday, but she would certainly not be running again so soon, particularly as that race was over seven furlongs. Neil Woolley went to see Tim en route to Ripon, and he had a good conversation with the trainer. For the first time, Tim hinted that she might not actually be good enough which caused some consternation, but I would prefer to draw a line under the Chester race, just as we had done with Star Of Lady M's disappointing run at the same course.

I searched the BHA website, and emailed Tim with the suggestion that either the stiff five furlongs at Beverley or six furlongs at Catterick might be her next options. In my mind, the way she moved to challenge at Thirsk showed that she had some ability, and many horses had failed to perform around the unique turns of Chester.

The following day, we received the Royal Ascot saddle cloth kindly sent to us from the racecourse. It was a fabulous memento of our day at racing's top table, and one that will be cherished. I also discovered, thanks to Simon Rowlands on Twitter, that Star Of Lady M had indeed run more than two seconds faster than she had ever run before at Goodwood. Her Musselburgh time was 59.76 seconds, whilst at Goodwood she completed the five furlongs in just 57.52 seconds. Even though Goodwood is a notoriously fast course, that was still a significant achievement and bodes well for the future.

So, we could relax with still eleven days until the Newbury race for Star Of Lady M. We agreed that we would drive down there on the morning of the race, and we booked our accommodation for a single night.

On Tuesday, our rating had dropped 1lb to 91, the same mark that had been given to Union Court. This was a surprise as many observers considered this to be her best performance so far. The Platinum Queen had been raised by eight to 106. There was an article online suggesting that The Platinum Queen may be supplemented for the Nunthorpe at York, though if they did not do this, she would still be at the Ebor meeting in the Julia Graves Roses Listed race. That would rule her out of the St Hugh's at Newbury, which was welcome news given her recent prowess. Emerald Duchess had been left on 54, as it was too early for an assessment of the Chester performance.

Chapter Thirty-Nine

With ten days until Newbury, I looked at what might happen afterwards. The Listed race at Ayr in mid-September was a possibility, as was the Group 3 race at Salisbury at the beginning of September. However, it looked like the Two-Year-Old Trophy at Ripon, a Listed race that often reduced down to a handful of runners, would be the best option. It was seventeen days after the Newbury race, so plenty of time for recovery.

The following day, I looked at the entries for the Phoenix Stakes at The Curragh. Miami Girl was entered, but it looked to be a particularly hot contest, with Little Big Bear, Persian Force and Bradsell all lining up. Miami Girl was duly withdrawn, and there were not many Class 1 or Class 2 races before the St Hugh's, which meant that we could face some stiff opposition.

On the Saturday that entries were due for the St Hugh's, they rose quite quickly. Beginning at ten, there were twenty by midday, and on paper they were a formidable bunch. Maylandsea, rated at 104, was the standout, but alongside her there was Miami Girl, Minnetonka and Katey Kontent all higher than ourselves. Union Court was also there, as was Carmela and Cuban Mistress both rated at 90. Further down the list there was Absolutelyflawless, but she was also entered into the nursery at the same meeting.

Later that day, the Phoenix Stakes took place at The Curragh. Blackbeard was withdrawn, but not before I realised that, like Star Of Lady M, he had also won four races this season. However, one of them was on the all-weather so I dismissed that. The race itself saw a very impressive performance from Little Big Bear, the winner of the Windsor Castle that we trailed fifteen lengths behind. It seemed that we were probably quite fortunate to get that close.

I assessed the St Hugh's entries. Clutching at my usual straws, I established that five of the runners were also entered in better quality races at York the following week, whilst four had alternative entries in lower class races. This, of course, meant nothing, but it would be nice to see one or two of the principals go elsewhere.

Two days later, two more alternative entries appeared, so there were eleven with other options as well as the St Hugh's, it would certainly be an interesting declarations stage on Wednesday.

On Tuesday, it was confirmed that Richard Hannon's Immortal Beauty was declared at Lingfield on Thursday, almost certainly reducing the field to a maximum of nineteen. However, two of the other alternative entries disappeared. I heard from my ever-growing grapevine that Maylandsea would probably run, and I did not think that was a bad thing. Her presence could certainly scare off some of the opposition.

The weather forecast for the day of the St Hugh's was a concern, with temperatures forecast to exceed thirty degrees. There was no sign of any rain in the south of the country, and there were concerns about field sizes from the clerks of the southern courses, including Newbury. It crossed my mind that during the previous week, the North had suffered several downpours, and perhaps that would give us an advantage as we had been able to keep our horse on the go. In the south, it was rumoured that only the all-weather gallops could be used because of the firm ground. A hosepipe ban confirmed the dire conditions south of Birmingham.

I also considered that maybe some of the entries would wait for the better ground at York the following week. These were just some of the endless possibilities that my mind conjured up to fill the void.

In Malton, Emerald Duchess was entered for the Class 6 nursery at Catterick the following Monday. Her rating had dropped to 51 following the Chester race. There were seventeen entries, and she was guaranteed a run if declared. To repeat a phrase that is perhaps on the defensive side, I could see no reason not to declare her.

Wednesday was the big day for the St Hugh's as it meant declarations. The message from Jason Kelly was simple enough, "She is up there in the ratings, and she is in good form, so let's declare." I agreed, and then we watched the entries tick up. This happened slowly at first, with only a solitary declared runner for quite some time. Eventually more came in, and the final figure of twelve was about what I expected. Treasure Trove was the only highly-rated horse that did not declare, so we would be up against Maylandsea, Katey Kontent, Minnetonka, Miami Girl and several other high-class fillies. Danny's original mount, Eternal Class, did not declare, but Danny was booked to ride in three races for David O'Meara at Thirsk. This was disappointing, but we were then delighted to secure the services of Jason Watson who had won on her at Musselburgh.

We were drawn in stall 4, much more central than our previous big race positions, so we could be confident of getting a reasonable position within the race. I hoped that the plan would be to track the early pace, and make our move with a furlong and a half to go.

We were initially priced up at 10/1 in the *Sporting Life* which was around seventh in the betting lists. William Hill opened with us at 14/1, a clear eighth best in their eyes. On the ratings we would do well to finish in the top six, but there were question marks against several of the runners. The *Sporting Life* only gave her two out of five stars. However, they did not dismiss her completely, simply suggesting that her third at Goodwood was from an unfavourable draw, and that she would need to improve for this Listed contest.

Temperatures were rising across the country again, but this time there was no doubt that the race would take place. By Thursday morning our travel plans were well advanced, and we could relax. The ROA gave my details to journalist and broadcaster, Nick Luck. He called me for an interview to feature in his podcast, and he seemed particularly interested in this book which will hopefully encourage racehorse ownership.

Meanwhile, the latest bill arrived from David O'Meara, and it was quite a big one. It had cost us almost £1,350 for our ultimately fruitless consideration of running in France. This was a Carnet charge, required to take goods, in this case Star Of Lady M and any associated kit, outside the UK. It had at least given us options. On the positive side, the Carnet should be valid for up to a year, so we could still race Star Of Lady M in France without paying again, or simply take her on holiday. The trips to Musselburgh and Goodwood had taken care of another £1,500, and that was without taking into account the jockeys' and entry fees. However, just like the prize money, all of this was quite incidental. She deserved her chance in these big races, and she had certainly earned the right, both in terms of performance and income.

Chapter Forty

I got an email from Tattersalls that the Book 3 sales catalogue was now available online. With twelve months experience since the last time that I looked at their catalogue, perhaps I would do a better job with my analysis this year. Only time would tell. It was a task for some quiet moments that would hopefully occur away from the track the following week.

On Friday morning, we set off early for Newbury racecourse, which was some three and a half hours away. Temperatures were steadily rising, with a forecast high of thirty-two. We arrived at Donnington Valley Hotel, and as our room was not ready, we had to change in the baking hot spa. It was still before midday, and we had time for a pint of the locally brewed lager in the bar. I think that it is fair to say that the locally brewed lager is best left to the locals.

I received a message from Jason Kelly stating that he was surprised at her odds that ranged from 20/1 to 25/1. He could not be there as he was at a wedding, but I suggested that the horse did not know what her odds were. There was some good news when the fancied Miami Girl was declared a non-runner, which squeezed our odds down to 18/1.

It was a short taxi ride to the course, where there was an easy check-in. The Owners Club was spacious and airy, with a cool breeze blowing through. Ten minutes after our arrival, we were tucking in to sea bass for lunch, in the relaxed atmosphere of the restaurant adjacent to the parade ring.

Sally and I had a look around and we were both impressed with Newbury. It struck me as a kind of "York of the South", with similarly spacious surroundings and plenty of outdoor seating areas.

The view from the grandstand was excellent, and we decided to watch the races from there. I looked at some form but to no avail, whilst Sally opted for the tried and trusted method of picking horses based on names. Hoof It Hoof It duly obliged at 20/1, but better was to come in the second race. Our eldest son is named Ole Joseph, and so Sally backed OJ Lifestyle. It just held on in a tight finish, at odds of 125/1. Even better, the Tote paid closer to 150/1, and so her £2 each-way bet returned almost £350.

The Owners Club was a friendly place, and we soon met Chris, part owner of Cobalt Blue that had finished just out of the frame, possibly due to the additional weight of the money that I had put on the horse. Chris was from Stockport, not too far from ourselves, and a few hundred miles away from Newbury, so there was an instant rapport. I filled the table with copious amounts of water, to combat the heat and my nerves that were starting to kick in. We chatted for quite some time. It was a welcome distraction, but my mind was really on Star Of Lady M. I could not concentrate on anything else, and I was quite relieved when it was time to go. She looked very well in the pre-parade ring, where her regular groom, Maddy, was looking after her, along with Sarah who we first met at Musselburgh.

As we entered the parade ring, I realised that the outsider, Queen Of Uplands, was also a non-runner, leaving just ten in the race. Incredibly, of the ten remaining runners, six were sired by the prolific Havana Grey, including, of course, Star Of Lady M.

Jason Watson was happy with her. It was a strong field, but we would see how the race panned out, and hope to challenge late. We headed for the stands as horse and rider headed for the start. She was still unfancied at 20/1, with Maylandsea the 5/2 favourite.

Star Of Lady M broke well, and was in behind Cuban Mistress and Union Court, with Minnetonka also up with the pace. Several of the fancied runners, including Maylandsea, Carmela and Katey Kontent, were soon under pressure. Woolhampton moved forward, and it seemed that Jason was struggling to find a way around Minnetonka. Cuban Mistress kicked again as Star Of Lady M saw daylight on the stands side. Jason pushed the button and she flew, gaining with every stride. Unfortunately, the line came too soon, and she finished fifth, just over two lengths off the winner. Union Court and Woolhampton filled the places, with Minnetonka a neck in front of us. With another fifty yards we could have reached third place, and with another one hundred we might even have got our head in front. Maylandsea, Carmela, Katey Kontent, and the much-vaunted Funny Story, were nowhere to be seen. Havana Grey had recorded an historic first and second.

It was a fabulous performance. In the parade ring afterwards, Star Of Lady M looked thrilled with her own efforts, and ready to go again. Maddy and Sarah were also delighted, but it was Jason Watson who gave the most detailed appraisal. He said that she would definitely get black type somewhere, it was only a matter of time. He also said that she made his job so easy as she was so genuine, running through the line.

I believed that she thoroughly enjoyed her race again, and she still had plenty of options. David O'Meara called and said that she had now proved that she could compete at Listed level. This gave us confidence to enter her in lots of races, but he was particularly interested in the Firth of Clyde at Ayr, which is a Listed race for fillies only over six furlongs. I mentioned the Two-Year-Old Trophy at Ripon, and he said that yes, of course that would be on the agenda. Luke called from Deauville, and he thought that all roads should lead to Ripon. We did not have too much time to chat as he was a little unsure of his whereabouts en route to Deauville, but we promised to meet up at York the following week.

Jason Kelly mentioned the Dick Poole at Salisbury, another Group 3 for fillies only, and the Firth of Clyde, but he also agreed that Ripon could be another possibility. He thought that we should spread our entries to keep options open. In the Owners Club we spoke to several of the Middleham Park Racing syndicate, owners of the winner, Cuban Mistress. They were a lively bunch, but very complimentary about Star Of Lady M, and they were interested in her name. I explained about Abraj Dubai, and of course Lady M, and one of them genuinely asked Sally if she preferred "Sally" or "Lady M". She laughed it off saying, "Sally's fine," and I thought that perhaps she was taking the "Lady M" part a little too much to heart.

Chapter Forty-One

We rose early the following day and made the long journey home. On arrival, we learned that Emerald Duchess had been declared to run at Catterick two days later, so I began the process of obtaining tickets. As I mentioned earlier, Edwina Currie was now a member of The 1891 Group syndicate, and she has taken in a family of Ukrainian refugees. She thought that it would be a great experience for them to attend a British race meeting, so I contacted Catterick who very kindly agreed to provide them with complimentary badges with lunch.

Richard Kent called and jokingly said that he felt honoured speaking to a celebrity. One of his friends from Ireland had called him and asked if he knows Mike Madden as he was speaking on the Nick Luck podcast. Richard was very complimentary, and made a fantastic suggestion of including a glossary in the book, to explain some of the common and perhaps obscure terms used in the racing industry.

I sat down and listened to the podcast, and it was fascinating. It is now another on my "podcasts to follow" list. I was featured towards the end, but it gave me the opportunity to hear views on the future of racing and several other pertinent topics.

Later that morning, Char-lee Heard messaged me from the yard to let me know that Star Of Lady M had once again come out of her race well, and she had trotted up sound.

I watched reruns of the race and with every viewing, I was more impressed. Then the demons kicked in. What if she did not get black type? What if we could not find a suitable race? What if she lost her form? All of our potential targets could be weak or strong, we would only know much nearer the time. Her TopSpeed of 69 was as mystifying as ever, and her RPR of 88 was perhaps a little less than I thought it would be. However, these meant precisely nothing, so I locked them away in the back of my mind and looked forward to the end of the month.

The Ripon race was still another sixteen days away. I could forget about Star Of Lady M until the entries were published six days in advance. In addition, after Monday's race, it would be several days before I would need to think about where Emerald Duchess might run next. It seemed as though I would be able to put our horses to the back of my mind for a while.

Of course, if you've read this far, then you will know things can change rather quickly, and in unexpected ways.

We set off for Catterick on the Monday morning, and as we pulled into the Owners & Trainers car park, I noticed a voicemail from Jason Kelly. He had entered Star Of Lady M into the Julia Graves Roses at York the following Saturday. This five-furlong Listed race is usually a competitive one, and although Jason thought that it might cut up if the anticipated rain fell and the going changed, I was not convinced. However, to have a runner at York was certainly on my bucket list. I had a quick scan of the entries, and it was just as I expected. Rocket Rodney led them with an OR of 105, closely followed by Crispy Cat with 104. There were also two rated at 99. The St Hugh's winner, Cuban Mistress, was included, as well as the fourth, Minnetonka, and sixth, Katey Kontent. In total, twelve of the entries were rated higher than Star Of Lady M.

At Catterick, there was great excitement. The racecourse has built a splendid new Owners & Trainers facility, and our Ukrainian guests soon settled down for lunch as they studied the racecards.

These must have made very little sense to them, but the boys in particular quickly found a winning formula. Edwina drew plenty of attention, including from the director of the racecourse.

We were in the second race, and as we entered the parade ring, I met Chris Dixon from RacingTV who was full of praise for Star Of Lady M. David O'Meara had a runner in our race, and another of Star Of Lady M's regular handlers, Di Jackson, came over to talk to us. She was amazed at how genuine and robust our filly was. She was impressed at how she came out of her races like it was nothing. However, we do know from our previous visit to the yard that she does like to stamp her authority at home.

Tim came into the ring, and as we waited for the syndicate to assemble, he spoke about Star Of Lady M in glowing terms. He was very impressed with her at Goodwood, though he had not yet seen the St Hugh's race. Everyone wanted to talk about Star Of Lady M, but it was time for Emerald Duchess.

David Allan was the day's jockey, and he was considered to be Tim's stable jockey. Tim was not sure what to make of Emerald Duchess, but that did not seem to concern David. We stressed that she had struggled leaving the stalls, but that she had shown some ability. He was very confident in what he was being asked to do, and this confidence spread throughout our party. Tim took time out to speak with Edwina, and then we made our way to the viewing area.

Emerald Duchess was drawn in stall 6 of the eleven runners, and she broke well. She was not leading, but she was certainly in the first six or seven. They reached the bend, and it all went wrong as she was bumped into. She had to be snatched up, and then it took David a while to get her balanced again. Coming out of the bend she had progressed up to fifth, but the effort in getting back on an even keel had clearly taken a lot out of her. She was eased down to finish ninth, and we went back to the parade ring for the post mortem.

David was very clear in his opinion that he was lucky to stay on board around the bend. It could have been a serious incident, and both rider and horse did well to come out of it safe and sound. The explanation given was that she had clipped the heels of the horse in front, but there were other factors that took away whatever chance she may have had. He thought that she did well, but that she was not a sprinter. She would do better over seven furlongs, and her hanging was not an issue. We should consider left or right-handed tracks. It was a very professional assessment, and despite the fading finish, we were pleased that she had put Chester behind her and shown some improvement.

I had a quick glance through the BHA website, and the next race that would be suitable for her, over the revised distance of seven furlongs, would be back at Catterick on the Wednesday of the following week, which just happened to be Ladies' Day.

Chapter Forty-Two

Tuesday was a day for ratings, and Star Of Lady M had surprisingly been dropped from 91 to 90. I thought that rather odd, as Minnetonka, who finished a neck in front of us, stayed at 94, and Carmela and Maylandsea, who were well behind, were also dropped by one to 89 and 103 respectively. It could have been an irritation, but I just considered that the BHA, and the *Racing Post* with the RPR, had once again underestimated her. She would surely prove them wrong.

Emerald Duchess was given a TopSpeed of just 3, but that was still better than the two who finished behind her. They did not even qualify for a rating. Her RPR was 34, and we were hopeful that she would be dropped a few more pounds when her next rating was announced.

On the day of the declarations for the Julia Graves Roses, I watched the numbers tick up. They surely went up too quickly for us to consider running, but I could not be certain until I spoke to Jason. As it turned out, the declarations closed with a total of ten, and we were not amongst them. Six of the runners were rated at 99 or above. Jason called and confirmed my thoughts that the field was just a bit too strong. He also said that the five furlongs at York would be very fast, and we really did need to try Star Of Lady M over six. So, it would be the following Tuesday when we made our next entry, for the Two-Year-Old Trophy at Ripon. I had considered that Catterick on 24th August might be appropriate for Emerald Duchess, but she was not entered for that. I suspected that Tim was waiting for her new handicap mark, so maybe Haydock in early September would be an appropriate target.

Chapter Forty-Three

Friday was the third day of the Ebor Festival at York, and although we did not have any official invitations, we ventured there anyway as we knew there would be plenty of people to meet. We arrived as the gates opened, and were immediately met by the ITV Racing paparazzi filming the early racegoers. The Champagne Pavilion seemed a good place to start, so we grabbed a table and settled in with a bottle of pink champagne. ITV Racing clearly thought this was a good idea too, as they filmed their introduction to the day using our champagne bucket and glasses as their starting point.

Luke Lillingston joined us, and he was full of enthusiasm for Star Of Lady M. Earlier that day, he had been to David O'Meara's yard with his Hot To Trot racing group, and David first brought out the Hot To Trot filly for them to look at. He followed this up by bringing out Star Of Lady M, and she looked a picture, in great condition and ready for her next race. We shared a few glasses of champagne and then wandered around the parade ring where, of course, Luke knew almost everyone.

Tim Easterby greeted us, and he explained that he had not entered Emerald Duchess into the Catterick race as he wanted to try her at a different track. This made sense, as we would not want her to relive the bad memories of what happened on that top bend. I met Nick Luck and he was very complimentary about Star Of Lady M's efforts at Newbury, reiterating his offer to feature us again on a future podcast. We also met Sam Hoskins, one of the partners in Hot To Trot, and he too was full of enthusiasm for Star Of Lady M. We watched The Platinum Queen finish a gallant second in the Group 1 Nunthorpe, an indirect compliment to Star Of Lady M as we had got within six lengths of that rival at Goodwood.

Finally, we met up with Simon Chappell who was sponsoring the fifth race on the card, and we spent a couple of hours chatting with him and his team. Simon has been a long-time owner of horses, but it seemed that the success of Star Of Lady M had tempted him into buying another two-year-old. It was a lovely feelgood kind of a day, with the majority recommending the Ripon race as our best opportunity for black type. This was based on Star Of Lady M having already won at the traditionally quirky course. Sam Hoskins did throw the wildcard of the Sirenia Stakes at Kempton into the mix. I thought that was an awfully long way to go for a compact all-weather contest, particularly as she did not act on the tight turns of Chester, albeit going in the opposite direction.

The following day, I nervously watched the entries for a seven-furlong handicap at Ffos Las. Fortunately, Emerald Duchess was not entered, and we would not have to endure the four-and-a-half-hour drive to the picturesque Welsh course.

Chapter Forty-Four

I narrowed down my search in the Tattersalls online Book 3 catalogue, and reduced the 299 fillies down to forty-two, all 100% GBB eligible. Havana Grey featured heavily, as you might expect, and I did wonder whether Lot 1910, another grey by the leading first season sire, might be at just the right point in the sale. However, based on last year, I realised that Luke would have a very different approach to selecting potential purchases.

By the end of Sunday, eight days before the Two-Year-Old Trophy at Ripon, I had analysed the previous runnings of the Ripon and Salisbury races, going back several years. I also looked at the latest BHA ratings, and I considered that of the six-furlong fillies, we had as good a chance as any. I was trying to convince myself, and of course, all of this research would ultimately count for nothing.

On Monday, I realised that the Somerville auction sales race was due to be run the following Saturday. This was not as valuable as our Tattersalls race on the 1st October, but it still had prize money of £100,000 and so should attract some of the runners that might otherwise be destined for Ripon or Salisbury. I looked down the entries and saw Eddie's Boy and Woolhampton, and perhaps a few of the lightly-raced challengers. This could only be a positive in advance of the Ripon entries being published the following day.

Tuesday morning began with an initial foray into the BHA website. Two entries for Ripon just after 8am. An hour later, there were still only three, and by 10am there were five. I guessed that maybe just over half of the final entries would actually be declared to run, so anything less than fifteen or sixteen would be good. As time ticked on into the final hour, the number reached seven, then eight and nine. With minutes to go, they finally reached double figures, and then the entries were closed.

It was around an hour later before they were officially published, and I spent quite some time analysing them. On the face of it, this would be a challenging target to get black type. There were five colts, including Al Karrar rated at 107 and Bolt Action at 97. Shouldvebeenaring won the Goffs sales race at York, and he was rated 92. The leading filly, Malrescia, was also on 92. At the lower end, Kitai did not yet have a rating, and Miss Mai Tai, who had finished fifth in the Hilary Needler, was on 72.

I did some more research, and the picture looked a little better. Al Karrar had the option of the Gimcrack at York but he ultimately opted for Ripon instead. Bolt Action would have very little time to recover from York, so perhaps he would go elsewhere. Shouldvebeenaring had to be nursed to his York race with sore shins, so perhaps he too would wait for another target farther down the line. Miss Mai Tai and Kitai had alternative engagements, potentially leaving just six runners. Of course, all of that was highly speculative, and likely to have no bearing on the final declarations. The next goal was to assess the entries for Salisbury on Friday, before we had to either declare for or scratch from the Ripon race the following day.

Chapter Forty-Five

The Goffs Premier Yearling Sale was well under way at Doncaster, and I kept a close eye on the Havana Grey progeny. I was surprised that on day one, the seven sold ranged from just 34,000 to 68,000 guineas. With the spectacular success of the first season sire, I thought that they would be closer to six figures. The following day, Havana Grey came to the fore when his daughter, a full sister to Katey Kontent, was bought for 230,000 guineas. This was where the thoroughbred industry used insight and guesswork to figure out if this latest filly would be better or worse than her sister, who only cost 65,000 as a yearling.

Meanwhile, it proved to be a good decision not to enter Emerald Duchess into the nursery at Catterick, as the meeting was abandoned before it would have taken place.

The Salisbury entries ticked up rather sharply, eventually totalling twenty-one. There were clearly many more than for the Ripon race, but I still considered Salisbury to be a potentially good option. As the Dick Poole was a fillies-only race, we would not have to worry about any highly-rated colts. The top-rated was Maria Branwell, the David O'Meara filly, who had a mark of 99. There were a few that had not yet qualified for a mark, but generally, the low to mid-nineties seemed to be the standard. I messaged Jason and we agreed to track the Ripon declarations the following morning before deciding which option to choose.

With the knowledge that there were more than twenty entries at Salisbury, which probably meant around twelve to fourteen runners, it would not take many withdrawals from the Ripon race to send us there. On Saturday morning, there was a slow start to declarations, and although I could see jockey nominations, I had begun to realise that they meant very little. Jason Watson was listed on board Star Of Lady M, and I saw that as the first positive sign that Ripon would be our destination. A short time later Jason Kelly confirmed this, and as 10am ticked around, the declarations closed at six. My original analysis, at the entry stage, proved to be completely off the mark. The three highest-rated colts were entered, but Malrescia was not. Miss Mai Tai was a surprise, having raced on Thursday, but she was rated considerably lower than us. We were fourth in the ratings, and we got a good draw in 5. To achieve black type, we had to confirm the ratings with Miss Mai Tai and Hoof It Hoof It, as well as beating one or more of Al Karrar, Bolt Action and Shouldvebeenaring. It looked certain that we would be able to renew acquaintances with the Middleham Park Racing members that we met at Newbury, as they had two runners in the race.

I looked at the purchase price of the other entries, and it showed the size of the gulf that we had to overcome. Figures of 180,000, 160,000 and 75,000 dwarfed our 15,000 guineas. However, Star Of Lady M had already shown that she deserved her place. The *Sporting Life* gave a good assessment of her chances, deciding that she was not out of things.

Chapter Forty-Six

The journey to Ripon was slightly delayed due to the Leeds Festival traffic, but we arrived shortly after noon. We were soon enjoying lunch in the Owners & Trainers bar. My youngest sister, Fiona, was with us, and we met my middle sister, Jane, when we got to the course. Her only previous experience of racing was when she watched Emerald Duchess make her debut at Nottingham. Jane had been following Star Of Lady M very closely. This was my fifth trip to a Yorkshire course as an owner that summer, and it was great to recognise some friendly faces on reception and in the bar. The staff rotated between the courses, ensuring that it was all run very efficiently as everyone knew what was expected of them.

It was a family fun day at Ripon and the course was very busy. It was also August Bank Holiday, which added to the numbers. The parade ring was three or four deep at times, and even the pre-parade ring was busy enough. I went for a walk to calm my nerves, and I spotted a few faces. These included Tim Easterby, and his travelling head lad, Geordie.

The favourite, Al Karrar, firmed up overnight to 1/2, but he began drifting. He went from odds-on to odds against, eventually going off at 11/8. Meanwhile, the two other colts were vying for second favouritism at around 3/1. We drifted throughout the morning, and at one point, the price of 25/1 was available. However, as the off time approached, we shortened quite dramatically, eventually starting as the 8/1 fourth favourite.

At the pre-parade ring, we chatted to Tim Easterby. He told us that he had sneaked black type in last year's race with Atomic Lady, and it made such a difference. He thought that the leaders had a tendency to go out too fast and cut each other's throats, giving the others a chance to take them late on. We also discussed Emerald Duchess, as he thought that perhaps she already needed a mile. I suggested the straight seven at Newcastle or Leicester might be a good next step, just to allow her to have a race where she did not hate the ground and did not have to fight her way around a bend. Tim agreed, but thought that Newcastle was a course that horses either love or hate. Perhaps that would be a complication she could do without. I also thought that we might be judging her too harshly, as her sire only ran three times as a two-year-old, and never at less than seven furlongs. I enjoyed the conversation, and although Tim had such a wealth of experience, he was very keen to listen to what I had to say.

We parted when David O'Meara appeared. Star Of Lady M trotted out, accompanied by her regular groom, Maddy, as well as head girl, Gabi. The previous week the stable had suffered a terrible tragedy when travelling head girl, Di Jackson, was involved in a head on collision after racing at Yarmouth. The horse, Lincoln Pride, sadly died in the accident, whilst Di suffered multiple injuries but was now on the long road to recovery. It was only a couple of weeks since Di came over to chat to us when Emerald Duchess raced at Catterick, and we very much felt that she was a part of our journey. Needless to say, she remains in our thoughts and prayers for a speedy recovery.

We were in the fourth race of the day, but I had managed to keep my nerves under control by chatting to Tim and David. As Star Of Lady M moved to the parade ring for her most important date so far, I could feel my mouth drying and my heartbeat quickening.

She looked in peak condition yet again. It really was remarkable that she seemed to thrive on her racing, even after a very long season. This was her ninth two-year-old race, and many others from her age group had not even seen a racecourse as yet.

In the parade ring, Jason Watson was confident. Even more so because he had just ridden a good winner in the previous race. He knew his job, but David reiterated that although we would be trying to win, first three would also be great for black type. At Newbury, Jason had told us that she would definitely get black type somewhere, but I did not remind him of that.

We moved to the stands and I realised that our friends from Middleham Park were not in attendance. I knew they were London-based, so I supposed that a Bank Holiday journey to Ripon was a stretch too far. As we took our seats, I could not look at anyone, and I could not speak. For a brief moment, the nerves were as highly strung as they had ever been, such was the importance of the task ahead.

The field moved behind the stalls, and as expected Star Of Lady M walked quietly in to her position. The plan was to break well enough to track the expected leader, Hoof It Hoof It, ahead of Miss Mai Tai on the rail. She could then make her move as the three colts pressed on the outside, and with the advantage of the rail, she might just see one or more of them off.

It did not quite work out like that. She got out well enough, behind the expected pace of Hoof It Hoof It. However, she moved across to the left, away from the rail, and bumped the favourite. Bolt Action took the leader on for pace, with Miss Mai Tai always struggling. We were in behind Shouldvebeenaring, and ahead of Al Karrar who quickly came under pressure. He did not find much, and as Hoof It Hoof It began to fade, we moved into third. Shouldvebeenaring forged ahead, with Bolt Action close behind.

Jason Watson eased our horse, confident that he would not catch the two in front, but more importantly that nothing else would catch him. Star Of Lady M finished a comfortable third, gaining black type in the process. She had only been beaten by two colts, seeing off the 107-rated favourite by a couple of lengths.

We were delighted. It was almost as emotional as that first win at Redcar. The nerves faded away as once again the adrenaline carried us along. We rushed to the parade ring, where David greeted us with a beaming smile after a job well done. The strange thing was that Jason reported that she hated the ground. Ripon could be quirky, and although she had won there before, she hit a few flat spots which slowed her momentum. This meant that she effectively had to start her charge all over again. With that in mind, it was an even more remarkable performance to get third, and it showed what an exemplary ride Jason had given her. He also told us that once again, she made his job easy for him, and that she was definitely the toughest filly that he had ever sat on. That was praise indeed.

David confirmed that Ayr should be the next target, and we discussed the 1st October races. That would be a tricky decision, but it did not have to be made just then. I got the BHA website up on my phone. David could not get a mobile signal, so I handed the phone to him. He looked at the entries for both the Tattersalls auction race at Newmarket and the Redcar Two-Year-Old Trophy. I noticed that Luke was calling, literally a couple of minutes after the race had finished. He must have been as excited as us, but I did not distract David from the important job in hand. We decided that we should stay in the Redcar race when the next stage came up the following week. The Newmarket race had no more stages until confirmations on 26th September.

I called Luke and he was understandably thrilled. He said that we should definitely visit Whitsbury Manor as part of the research for this book, and Ed Harper would be very pleased to see us. His Havana Grey had sired both the first and third in the prestigious Ripon Two-Year-Old Trophy, and Whitsbury Manor was the birthplace of our girl, as well as the home of her mother, Abraj Dubai. Abraj Dubai had since had another yearling by Showcasing, and was currently nursing her latest foal by Sergei Prokofiev. We would definitely have visited Whitsbury Manor if we had opted for the Salisbury race rather than Ripon, but now we would have to make a special trip.

The congratulations came thick and fast, including from Richard Kent, Jason Kelly, Simon Chappell and Mike Curtis. We met Tim Easterby coming out of the Owners & Trainers bar and he offered his congratulations. He had a wide grin and he was obviously and genuinely pleased for us. We sat down for a celebratory drink, which was largely soft due to the long journey home.

It was a surreal feeling. I discussed insurance with Luke, and he thought that £100,000 was just about enough, but no one would argue if we wanted to increase it slightly. We had an exciting autumn ahead of us, but in some respects, the pressure had been taken off us. We had achieved the holy grail of black type.

Epilogue

Part One

As often happens, the next race at Ripon passed us by, but we went into the grandstand to watch the sixth. I noticed a missed call from David O'Meara, so I called him back and he gave me some worrying news. Star Of Lady M had sustained a cut during the race. It was nothing to worry about, but it was quite deep and close to the tendon. So, he wanted to take her to his vet where it would be flushed out properly. He would let us know how she was tomorrow. This dampened down our euphoria somewhat, but we knew that she was in the best hands. The Ayr race was nineteen days away, and I could not help wondering if she would still go for that, or indeed race again at all this season. Her health must be the priority.

After a long drive home, I went through all of my messages. I then caught up with the Weighed In racing podcast. This is a very good listen, and it features Kevin Blake who I think talks a lot of sense about all things racing. Towards the end a question was put to the panel. "Should black type be restricted to standard place rules?" If that was the case, then Star Of Lady M would have missed out, having finished third of six. Kevin's somewhat controversial view was that black type should be scrapped. He qualified this by stating that ratings are the only true guide, but I had to disagree. I found the ratings quite subjective, and they did not take into account all aspects of a horse's performance. Black type might not be perfect, but it was awarded in specific races that have proven their quality over several years. The place rules were to simplify the whole process, I guess, and I was certainly not complaining about it.

The following morning, the news was better. The vet had done a white blood cell count which had come back normal. This suggested that there was no infection. The wound had been flushed out and stitched, and David expected Star Of Lady M to return home later that day or the following morning.

I put it to the back of my mind as I focused on two pieces of news. Firstly, Star Of Lady M had been given a TopSpeed rating of 76, which was her second highest ever. Her highest was 80, also gained at Ripon. Secondly, Emerald Duchess had been entered into the seven-furlong nursery at Newcastle, along with twenty-three other runners. I had emailed Tim with my thoughts on Newcastle and Leicester, and suggested that other targets could be Redcar over a mile in three weeks' time, as well as nurseries at Chepstow, Musselburgh and Leicester again. The nurseries were certainly attracting a lot of entries, so I suggested a maiden at Nottingham might also be an option. He came back to me quickly, confirming that he would also enter her at Leicester. However, he would be keeping an eye on the weather as we would not want to run her if it was too soft.

Later that day, David called again, and this time, the news was not so good. They had done a second white blood cell count and it was slightly up. This was a worry because of the chance of sepsis, so they had given her an anaesthetic and flushed out the joint again. At times like this, a lack of knowledge could create demons in your mind and problems could grow out of all proportion. I was very worried, but David said that she would be fine, and Luke suggested that it did not sound too serious. I could not begin to think about other races, I just wanted some positive news.

The Listed Salisbury race looked to be of decent quality, with David's Maria Branwell installed as the early favourite. Her rating of 99 was above all of the others. There were twelve entries in total, and it looked to be a competitive renewal.

The following day, I waited until early afternoon, when I confirmed that Emerald Duchess had been entered into the nursery at Leicester along with seventeen others. It was a 0-65 event, and I noticed that two of the entries were rated 70 and 72, so surely, they must be eliminated?

With twenty-four entered at Newcastle, and a maximum field size of just fourteen, there would probably have to be some eliminations. The elimination sequence was published and we were not on it. If we wanted to run there, we would definitely get in, but my mind was elsewhere.

The hours ticked by on Wednesday afternoon, and there was still no update. I knew that David would be short-staffed and I did not want to bother him, so I contented myself that no news must be good news. The RPR was published, and we were given 87. I thought we might have been a little higher, with the first two being rated at 105 and 101. However, I guess the fact that we got the fillies weight allowance, coupled with Jason easing her down, meant that we could not really be given any higher. As with the TopSpeed, these were just nominal figures that did not really mean anything.

On Thursday, it was confirmed that two of the Leicester entries had not qualified as their rating was too high. I was thinking of Willow Farm. I messaged David for an update, and his response was reassuring. The surgery had gone well, she was up and about, and they would keep her at the vets for a couple of days before sending her home. In my mind, that was Saturday, but in reality, I knew that this was imprecise. It could be Friday, or it could be early next week. I would just have to wait. David also sent a picture of the wound which looked horrific. However, it was just a flesh wound. He reiterated that she would be fine, and Luke again thought that it was not too serious. Perhaps she could run in a boot? I contented myself in simply hoping that she came back to the stable safe and sound.

On Saturday morning, I had a conversation with Tim. We decided that we would not run at Newcastle, as the surface would introduce yet another variable to the career of Emerald Duchess. Leicester would be a much more straightforward option. When the declarations came out on Sunday, she was drawn in stall 2 of ten, with Cam Hardie on board. A bit of research told me that Cam had a 3% strike rate for two-year-olds on turf, but I was not going to let that worry me.

The Newcastle race ended up with fourteen runners, so we had at least given ourselves the best chance numerically.

On Monday morning, I received the news that Star Of Lady M would be heading home later that day. She had been with the vet for a week, but I reassured myself that it was all precautionary. I did not sound convincing. The following day she was given a rating of 88, which was down another 2lbs. I thought that was bizarre after finishing third in a Listed race, and again, it was probably her best run to date. Shouldvebeenaring was rated at 101 with Bolt Action at 100. Even with the fillies' allowance, I thought that we might have been closer to that pair. Perhaps the official handicapper wanted to push us towards handicaps again.

The Redcar Two-Year-Old Trophy field reduced by ninety-nine, leaving just ninety-four entries. We were still one of them, and we had paid the additional £200, which was the first sure sign that we would be racing again in the not-too-distant future. Many of the big guns, including Wodao and Persian Force, were no longer entered at Redcar. The Tattersalls auction race had reduced by eight, leaving 160 still in.

On the day of the Leicester race the post arrived early, and it included Tim's latest bill. Two entries puzzled us, a scope from the vet, and a physio treatment. I made a mental note to ask whoever accompanied the horse when we reached the racecourse.

We set off for Leicester and immediately hit traffic problems. A truck had jack-knifed across a country lane in our village, but after a short delay we continued on our way. It was a pleasant day, and the expected rain had not really arrived. There were a few showers, but the going was still officially Good. Emerald Duchess was available at 40/1, and with some bookmakers paying an extra place, it felt like a reasonable bet. The pundits did not seem to give her much chance, but we certainly did. We had a plan, which they were blissfully unaware of.

As race time approached, we were in good spirits, having backed a previous winner at around 9/1. Luke Lillingston's Hot To Trot group had also had a winner when Rage Of Bamby won the next, and after listening to the presentation we headed to the pre-parade area. We met Rory from Tim's yard, and he had travelled there alone. He invited us into the stable, where Emerald Duchess was having the final few adjustments made to her tack prior to the race. She looked well, and she was happy to have us alongside her. She was still quite small, but we knew she had plenty of scope for growing into her racing career.

Rory clarified that the bill would be just routine. Nothing more serious than a runny nose, as two-year-olds could be like schoolchildren; when one of them caught an illness they all got it. There was nothing to be worried about, and Tim clearly did not think it was serious enough to alert us. I guess that if he had to inform every owner of every little ailment or procedure, he would never be off the phone.

Rory was very particular about where Emerald Duchess went into the parade ring. He waited until he could be sure that she would parade behind a filly as opposed to a colt. I had not seen this before, but I was certainly impressed by his attention to detail. We met Cam Hardie in the parade ring, and he was a confident young jockey. He had been in to Tim's to ride Emerald Duchess at home, and he was pleased with her. Rory said that she certainly performs better than a 51 at home, we just had to try to unlock that ability on the course. Cam exuded confidence, and said that we would hopefully learn some more about her over the challenging seven furlongs. He said that he had been riding out on the course. It was riding Good to Soft, which should be just fine.

We went towards the stands, accompanied by Rory. As we had been successful so far that day, we took him to our lucky spot about half a furlong from the finish. Superstitions could count for a lot when you were seeking a change of fortune.

As the race began, Emerald Duchess got out well. After three furlongs, she was being ridden, seemingly outpaced. She was under pressure, and then she started to find something. Menalippe and River Usk went clear, but Emerald Duchess flew after them. She was a fast finishing third at the line, easily her best position so far. We were all delighted, and Rory immediately announced that she would be even better over a mile. Cam came back and said exactly the same, although he also said she stumbled on the uneven ground, and so a flatter track might also suit. In my mind I had already identified a race at Redcar later in the month that seemed to fit the bill.

Rory disappeared to look after the horse, and we bumped into Cam again a short time later. He had spoken to Tim and they agreed that the mile at Redcar would be a great opportunity. Luke called, and he was more relieved than anything. He always had faith in her, and now she had shown that she does have ability and we could look forward to a bright future with her.

The commentator praised the front two and was quite dismissive of the rest of the field. However, he did counter this by opining that at least Emerald Duchess showed something, running past the rest of the field. She was given a TopSpeed of 35 and an RPR of 42. These were the lowest of all of the field. Her OR was dropped one to 50, but all of that meant nothing to us.

After four troubling months and five inconclusive runs, our plan was finally starting to come together. I was so pleased for the syndicate, even though there were just two of us at Leicester. We could look forward to the rest of the season, as well as her three-year-old career, with renewed confidence.

Part Two

The sales season was in full swing, and at the Tattersalls Somerville Sale the half-sister to Star Of Lady M was sold for 52,000 guineas. This was a full sister to Aye Catcher, Abraj Dubai's first foal that was rated at 66. It seemed reasonable to assume that Star Of Lady M's prowess would have had some effect on the purchase price.

I had not heard any more from David, but I was content that the additional payment had been made for Redcar, and she would probably be settling in back at home.

On Thursday morning, that all changed. I received a picture message from David that was the vet's report for Star Of Lady M. It was in tiny print, and before I had chance to read it I received a voicemail, also from David.

"Hiya Mike. There is a vet note for Star Of Lady M. A lot of it will be in vet speak which, if you're not used it, can be a little bit mind boggling. Ultimately, the prognosis is good but the filly is finished for this year. She just needs a bit of time now for the wound to heal up, and everything to settle down. It was a nasty cut, but she's fine."

I was gutted, and I felt kind of empty. No more nerves, no more excitement, no more scanning the Listed races on the BHA website, and no more assessing entries. My first thought was that it must be serious if she could not be ready to race by the end of October. I listened to the message again, and then several more times. I let David's words sink in, and I realised that whatever the injury was, she was in the best place.

I read the report in full, and the prognosis was indeed good. The stitches would come out four days later, and she would need four weeks of box rest. This would be followed by four weeks in a small paddock and then four weeks in a large paddock. If she came through all of that OK, she would be able to resume training. That would take us to December, so any thought of running before the start of the next flat season could be pushed aside.

The following day, I received a picture from David showing a remarkable recovery from the original gash. It looked so good that Luke thought that she might recover earlier, but that was not the case. We discussed her recuperation and what a three-year-old career might look like for her. He mentioned the Kilvington at Newmarket, and there was also the Commonwealth Cup Trial at Ascot. Both seemed an awfully long time away. It would probably be around two hundred days before she saw a racecourse again.

I then reflected on where she had taken us. Royal Ascot, Glorious Goodwood, Chester, Newbury, as well as her victories at

Redcar, Ripon, Beverley and Musselburgh. Her season culminated in getting black type at Ripon, and she deserved a rest. She would be at home at Willow Farm until the spring, when we could hopefully look forward to her three-year-old career. She was the first winner of the season for her sire, Havana Grey, and for her trainer, David O'Meara. Could she repeat that in 2023?

Part Three

We crossed Ayr off the calendar, but decided to make the most of the time by arranging a trip to Whitsbury Manor near Salisbury. It was a long drive, and we decided to break up the journey by stopping off at Stonehenge on the way. Neither Sally nor myself had ever seen it in person, and it is what you would expect. Ancient stones arranged in a vague circle. That evening, we stayed at the Three Lions at Fordingbridge. It was an excellent pub and restaurant with rooms that included a hot tub. Suitably refreshed, we nipped to Bournemouth Beach the following morning, and then after breakfast we headed to Whitsbury. This magnificent stud farm is home to Havana Grey and Abraj Dubai, both of Star Of Lady M's parents.

We went into the office and they were very excited to see us. They had been following Star Of Lady M's career with interest, and although they were disappointed to hear of her injury, they knew that she was tough enough to overcome such a setback. We had met Phil and Chris at the sales, and they tongue-in-cheek commented that it gave them much more satisfaction selling Star Of Lady M to us for 15,000 guineas, than getting half a million from a big organisation; it was obvious at the time just how excited we were to take ownership of the filly.

It was a busy time for the farm, preparing yearlings and foals for the upcoming sales, but Ed Harper drove us around to see all of his stallions. I expected them to be huge, unruly beasts, but Havana Grey was calm as his handler paraded him. He looked us up and down, wondering what all of the fuss was about. Abraj Dubai was out in a paddock with her latest foal by Sergei Prokofiev. Ed warned us that she could be a bit of a madam, but her inquisitive nature worked in our favour as she walked across to the fence to see who her visitors were. She loved a head scratch, and her foal eyed us up and down, gaining confidence from its mother.

When it was time to go, we thanked them all and said that we would hopefully catch up at the sales. We had seen stallions, mares, foals and yearlings, and who knows, we may even have seen the next Star Of Lady M.

Glossary

The Sales

Sales are usually undertaken at one of the major auction houses. There are sales of foals, yearlings, mares, horses in training, etc. Sales catalogues are available online, and it is now possible to bid online rather than attending the sales in person.

Guinea

A guinea is an old English term for a unit of currency equivalent to one pound and one shilling. In today's currency that would be £1.05. The guinea is the standard unit of currency used at the racehorse sales, with the shilling, or 5p, being the 5% commission charged by the auction house.

Arqana

Deauville based thoroughbred auction house.

Goffs

Thoroughbred auction house with multiple locations across Ireland and the UK.

Tattersalls

Thoroughbred auction house with multiple locations across Ireland and the UK.

Breeze Ups

These are sales for unraced two-year-olds. The horses have generally been bought as yearlings, and they are sold after having a two-furlong gallop on a racecourse. This gives the opportunity to see the two-year-old in action ahead of any potential purchase.

Horses In Training

This sale is exactly as it says. Horses offered for sale are already in training, giving potential buyers a horse that is generally ready to race.

Pinhook

The idea of a pinhook is to purchase a horse as a foal and sell it for profit as a yearling.

The Ratings

Timeform

Timeform is considered to be one of the best rating systems in the industry; however, the ratings are hidden behind a paywall. As well as the ratings, Timeform provides a symbol and flag system which provides additional information such as horses which should improve, or which are unreliable.

TopSpeed

TopSpeed rating is based on a horse's speed. It appears alongside other ratings in the *Racing Post*. It should be noted that the TS rating on a racecard is adjusted for weight. Different ratings are given based on whether the horse races on turf or all-weather.

Racing Post Rating (RPR)

The RPR appears a day or two after a race. Each horse is given a rating based on their performance. However, the initial RPR often changes in the days and weeks after it is first published. It should be noted that the RPR on a racecard is adjusted for weight. Different ratings are given based on whether the horse races on turf or all-weather.

Official Rating (OR)

The ORs are issued by the BHA (see below). A horse receives an OR once it has raced three times. However, the first ORs for two-year-olds appear towards the end of June. The OR is updated every Tuesday for any horses that have run in the preceding week.

The Organisations

British Horseracing Authority (BHA)

The BHA is responsible for the governance, regulation and administration of British horseracing. They provide a racing administration website where owners can see their own horses, ratings, colours, sponsorships, entries, etc. This site also has a search tool for every horse race on the British racing calendar, and a list of current entries and declarations.

Weatherbys

Weatherbys administer British racing on behalf of the BHA, which sometimes makes it confusing as to which organisation you are actually dealing with. They will often have the same telephone numbers and email addresses. Weatherbys also provide banking services. With a Weatherbys racing bank account, all of an owner's racing expenses and prize money can be managed automatically.

Jockey Club

The largest horseracing organisation in the UK. It owns several racecourses as well as the National Stud. The Jockey Club previously held a governing role within the sport but much of that has now been divested to the BHA.

Racehorse Owners Association (ROA)

The ROA was established to promote and protect the interests of racehorse owners. The ROA offers many member benefits and plays a key role throughout the racing industry.

Timeform

Data and content provider for horseracing. Its ratings are often seen as industry standard.

Sporting Life

Originally a horseracing newspaper but now a multi-media horseracing and other sports content provider.

Racing Post

Multi-media horseracing and other sports content provider. Also produces its own ratings (RPR).

Attheraces

Multi-media horseracing content provider. Also now branded as Sky Sports Racing.

The Race

Entries

A horse must be officially entered into a race before it can compete. Entries are generally done by the trainer. For most races, the entries close at midday, six days before the race. However, no entries are published on Sundays, and so Mondays tend to be busy, with entries to be completed for the following Saturday and Sunday. Each entry commands a fee, and these can vary dramatically. Lower class races can be just a few pounds, whereas Group races can run into thousands.

There are also Early Closing races, where the entry is done in a number of stages. There will be an initial entry fee, and then at the next stage the horse can either be scratched or an additional entry fee will become due. There can be several stages before finally getting to declarations.

Declarations

Declarations must be made by 10am two days before a race. The declaration is made by the trainer, which effectively means that they intend to run the horse in the race. In some instances, a horse may be balloted out of a race if the maximum field size is exceeded. In other instances, a race may divide into two, ensuring that more of the declarations can actually run.

Handicap

In a handicap race, the horses are allotted weight according to their OR. If a horse wins after the weights are published, it will carry an additional penalty.

Nursery

This is the term for a handicap race for two-year-olds.

Sales Race

A Sales Race is a race restricted to horses sold at a particular auction. For instance, the Tattersalls October Auction Stakes is restricted to horses purchased in the Tattersalls Somerville Yearling Sale or the

Tattersalls Yearling Sales (Book 3 and Book 4). Sales races are generally Early Closing races, with the initial entry being several months before the actual race.

Bumper

This is a flat race but run under National Hunt rules, so there are no obstacles and the race is not started from starting stalls.

Conditions Race

This is a race in which the weight each horse carries is determined by the conditions of the race rather than by its handicap mark. Variables could be sex, age, previous wins, etc.

Class

Races are divided into Classes, with Class 6 being the lowest grade and Class 1 the highest. The Class is separate from the type of race, eg Selling, Handicap, Novice, etc.

Class 1

Class 1 races are further subdivided into Group 1 (the highest quality), Group 2, Group 3 and Listed. These races are reviewed annually and can move up or down their designated category.

Pattern Races

Group 1, 2 and 3 races are collectively known as Pattern races.

Claiming Race

In a Claiming Race, all of the runners can be claimed after the race for a price set by the trainer at the entry stage.

Selling Race

In a Selling Race, the winner is auctioned off at the racecourse. In addition, any of the other runners can be claimed after the race for a price set by the trainer at the entry stage.

Maiden Race

Restricted to horses that have not previously won a race.

Novice Race

Restricted to horses that have not previously won more than two races.

Black Type

This refers to the black type in a pedigree, typically seen in a sales catalogue. The term "Black Type" refers to the text being in black type which makes it stand out on a page. To achieve black type, a horse must be placed in a Listed or Group race. If a horse wins a Listed or Group race, then the black type is also capitalised.

Stakes Race

A Listed or Group race.

Apprentice Race

A race in which all of the riders must be apprentices.

Winning Distances

Winning distances are measured in lengths, which equates to the length of a horse. A length can be subdivided into a quarter, half and three quarters of a length. In addition, shorter distances can be described as a nose, a short head, a head, or a neck.

Going

The going is an important factor in any horse race, and there are measurements and terms that describe the different conditions that the ground can be in.

Going Stick

The Going Stick is a device used to guide the Clerk of the Course as to the state of the ground. The stick is inserted into the ground to take a reading. Another reading is taken of the force required to pull the stick to a 45 degree angle. The readings are taken in several places, and therefore the going can vary. For example, it could be described as Good, Good to Firm in places. It should be noted that the Going Stick readings and the description given by the Clerk of the Course are independent of each other, though obviously, they are closely aligned.

Firm

Equivalent to a Going Stick reading of 9.9.

Good to Firm

Equivalent to a Going Stick reading of 8.6.

Good

Equivalent to a Going Stick reading of 7.9.

Good to Soft

Equivalent to a Going Stick reading of 7.1.

Soft

Equivalent to a Going Stick reading of 6.4.

Heavy

Equivalent to a Going Stick reading of 5.7.

Head Gear

Blinkers

Cups placed at the side of the horse's eyes to prevent the horse from being distracted and to help it to concentrate on what is ahead.

Visor

Similar to blinkers but with a cut in the side allowing the horse to have some peripheral vision.

Tongue Tie

A piece of elastic or nylon used to tie the tongue in place. This is to prevent the tongue from blocking the airways.

Red Hood

This can be fitted to a horse prior to a race to cut down noise, with the aim of reducing stress and keeping the horse calm. It can only be worn before the start of a race, and not during the race itself.

Hood

A hood of any colour other than red can be worn during a race. The aim is to reduce noise and prevent the horse from becoming nervous or distracted.

Cheekpieces

These are fitted to the horse's head stretching from the ear to the mouth. They have the same purpose as blinkers, to prevent the horse from being distracted and to help it to concentrate on what is ahead.

Noseband

These visible bands are placed on a horse to improve its concentration. It helps the horse to look down towards the noseband rather than to maintain a high head carriage.

The Horse

Foal

A young horse less than one year old. The term applies whether the horse is male or female.

Colt

A young male horse.

Gelding

A male horse that has been castrated.

Filly

A young female horse.

Mare

An adult female horse.

Maiden

A horse that has yet to win a race.

Novice

A horse that has not won more than two flat races and has not won a Class 1 flat race (there are several nuances to this).

Wind Operation

A procedure designed to improve the airflow of a horse during a race.

Sore Shins

Frequent ailment of two-year-olds, often associated with over-training, but this is not always the case. Evidenced by heat and pain in the front of the leg, sore shins are usually treated with a reduced workload.

Genuine

Generally means a horse that will always give its maximum effort when asked to do so.

Uncomplicated

A racehorse that has few quirks and will do as asked.

Sire

The father.

Dam

The mother.

Damsire

The sire of the dam of the horse, the maternal grandfather.

Conformation

This refers to the shape and structure of a horse and can have a significant effect on its ability and sale price.

Condition

A horse carrying condition means that it is fit and ready to race, with well-toned muscles. A horse carrying too much condition can be described as overweight and therefore unfit. However, this is not an exact correlation.

Name

A racehorse must be registered with a unique name. It cannot be longer than eighteen characters, and the only punctuation allowed is an apostrophe. Names are not allowed to contain more than seven syllables, and names in dubious taste are not permitted. There is a name generator on the BHA website. Once a suitable name is found, it must be submitted to the BHA for approval.

Ran Green

A horse that ran green showed its inexperience and immaturity, often by hanging to one particular side, or misbehaving before or during the race.

Exposed

An exposed horse has already raced several times and is unlikely to show significant improvement.

On the Bridle

This term is used when a horse is under control and travelling well in a race.

Off the Bridle

This term is used when a horse is not travelling well and is under pressure in a race.

Cut

Describes ground that is not firm. For example, a horse that likes cut in the ground would prefer softer ground. It can also be described as a horse that likes to get his hooves in, which means the same thing.

Hooves Rattle

A horse that likes to hear his hooves rattle indicates that he likes firm ground, referring to the noise the hooves make when encountering firm or hard ground.

The Course

Pre-Parade Ring

Most, but not all, courses have a pre-parade ring. This is where you will probably first see your horse at the racecourse. They may be led around unsaddled at first to get them used to their surroundings. Once saddled and ready to go, they will progress to the parade ring.

Parade Ring

This is where the punters get their first look at the horses. They are led around, and the crowd can be in close proximity. The trainer or trainer's representative will be in the parade ring, giving last minute instructions to the jockey and explaining the tactics to the owner.

Draw

Flat races are started from starting stalls, numbered in accordance with however many runners there are in the race. The runners are drawn at random to see which horse goes into which stall. The draw takes place shortly after the final declarations are published, generally two days before the race.

Draw Bias

This term is used to indicate whether one side of the draw is more favourable compared to the other side. For instance, is it better to have a high draw or a low draw? Some courses have a distinct draw bias, others have no draw bias. It is possible that the draw bias can be different depending upon the going as well as the race distance. Another factor is the size of the field, i.e. the number of runners in the race. A seven-runner race may show no draw bias, but a twenty-runner race may favour one side or the other.

Horses for Courses

A "C" next to a horse's name in the racecard means that it has won at that course before. When it is denominated as "CD" it means that the horse has won at the course and over the distance of this latest race. Some horses thrive at certain courses and become known as course specialists.

Furlong

Races in the UK are measured in furlongs, an imperial measurement equal to 220 yards. When a race does not fit into an exact number of furlongs, the additional distance is measured in yards.

All-Weather Surfaces

There are six all-weather racecourses in the UK. Three race on Polytrack and three on Tapeta. The surfaces are sufficiently different to turf that some organisations produce separate statistics for performances on all-weather and turf.

Start Position

Every track has a map detailing the start position for every race. Five-furlong races are frequently straight, but there are exceptions such as at Chester and Kempton. Some racecourses employ chutes to extend a straight part of the course, giving a start position that is not a part of the main circuit.

Photography

Every course has an accredited photographer. You will certainly notice them around the Winners' enclosure, and if you are fortunate enough to win, they will probably give you a business card directing you to their website. They usually have a lot of photos that you can purchase in various formats and sizes, both of the presentation and the race itself.

The Owner

Colours

As an owner you can select your own racing colours or silks. It is possible to customise your own silks. There is a handy tool on the BHA website that allows you to design your own silks, using a given set of colours and patterns. The tool will also tell you if your chosen design is already in use. You must register your colours, and you must get a set of silks made, although the trainer can arrange this.

Purchase Price

If you buy your horse at the sales, you have to make arrangements for payment, generally within thirty days of the sale.

Wind Test

After your purchase, and before the sale can be considered final, the horse must undergo a wind test at the auction house. This involves the horse running in both directions in a circle whilst a vet listens for any abnormalities in their breathing. There is a fee to be paid to the vet for this test.

Transport

There will be one or more transport companies at the auction house, and you must arrange for the horse to be transported from the sales to your trainer, usually the following day. There will be a fee to pay to the transport company for this service.

Insurance

As an ROA member there is insurance in place at "fall of hammer" at the sales. However, you are well advised to obtain full insurance from one of the many firms that offer this service. You should also bear in mind that if your horse is lucky enough to win races, you may need to consider increasing your insurance coverage.

Racing Fees

As an owner it is advisable to open a Weatherbys bank account. This enables all BHA fees, some of which are detailed below, to be deducted automatically. In addition, any prize money, appearance money, bonuses, etc will be automatically credited.

Entry Fees

Every race requires one or more entry fees, and in general these are due regardless of whether a horse actually runs. Entry fees are a BHA transaction and will be automatically deducted from your Weatherbys bank account.

Jockey Fees

The jockey fee is standard and may be subject to VAT.

Sponsorship

Horses can be sponsored and there are many ways to do this. Many trainers have sponsorship schemes, as do the ROA and Weatherbys. You can also get a private company to sponsor your horse. The sponsorship scheme must be approved by Weatherbys. Once it is approved, the sponsor's logo must appear in one or more of the recognised advertising areas on a jockey's silks, or the saddle cloth.

VAT

If you have an approved sponsorship, you can register for VAT. VAT can be reclaimed on all applicable racing expenses, including some travel and accommodation costs. Weatherbys and the ROA provide a VAT service. However, if you already have a company accountant, they will probably be able to produce your VAT returns. If you use Weatherbys VAT service, their fee will automatically be deducted from your account.

Great British Bonus (GBB)

A scheme that incentivises and rewards the breeding, buying and racing of British bred fillies by awarding bonuses up to £20,000 per race. The bonus is shared by the owner, breeder, trainer, jockey and stable.

Training Fees

Trainers normally bill monthly, and the bills can vary from trainer to trainer. The biggest item will be the monthly training fee, usually broken down to a daily rate. However, the daily rate can cover a variety of charges, and some trainers prefer to itemise charges separately.

Transport

Most trainers charge a mileage fee for transporting a horse to the racecourse.

Expenses

Staff expenses are incurred when your horse runs. If the racecourse is some distance away, then the horse will sometimes travel the day before which will incur additional staff expenses.

Stalls Training

Stalls training requires several people in attendance and will sometimes be charged separately.

Farrier

The farrier bill will normally be included in the monthly bill.

Plating

This applies when your horse actually races. The fitting of racing plates is sometimes an explicit item on your bill, though it can also be included within the farrier fees.

Dentist

Dentistry will often be itemised on the monthly trainer's bill.

Feed Supplement

This is over and above the daily training fees and comes to around £15 per month.

Drugs

Miscellaneous drugs are a staple of the monthly bill but should only be around £15.

Electrolytes

Electrolytes are usually administered on a race-by-race basis incurring a small charge of around £5. This is to replace salts, etc. that may be lost through sweating.

Gallops

Some trainers charge an additional fee for gallops, particularly where the trainer uses shared gallops.

Veterinary Bills

The vet bills can be included in the monthly bill, or in some cases can be invoiced to you directly by the vet.

Foreign Charges

If you ever race abroad, then your trainer will normally do all of the administration. The registrations will appear within your Weatherbys bank account, but the race entry charges will be billed through your monthly trainer's bill.

Owners Hospitality

One of the major benefits of being an owner is being able to see your horse race. Each time it is declared you will be entitled to around six badges plus lunch. This varies from course to course, and it is usually possible to order additional badges and lunch vouchers for a reasonable charge. Most of this can be achieved through the RCA Pass system, which is explained on the ROA website.

The Trainer

Having a working relationship with your trainer is very important and will significantly increase your enjoyment of racehorse ownership.

Communication

Some trainers communicate more than others. At the beginning, you will not know what you think should be communicated and what you are not interested in. Do you really want to know the ins and outs of every piece of dentistry? The one thing that I have found is that you should speak to your trainer. They will always listen. And do not be afraid to make suggestions. They will soon get to know how much involvement you want.

Visits

Seeing your horse at the yard is another great way to enhance your racehorse ownership, and to get to know your trainer and their team. It is highly recommended that you make arrangements in advance, and that you choose a suitable time when you can see your horse on the gallops. In general, the horses go out on the gallops in "lots", and if the trainer knows that you are arriving at a certain time, he can ensure that your horse goes out in the appropriate lot.

Options

A trainer will want to give your horse options. For instance, there may be two or three races within a day or so of each other, and they will want to give your horse the best chance of winning. This could be based on expected going, other entries, or several other factors. Therefore, you can find that your horse is entered into more than one race, and the additional entry fees are effectively lost. This does not make much difference in the Class 5 maidens or novice races, but the entry fees can mount up for better quality races. However, this is the same for everyone, and by giving your horse different options you will hopefully increase your chances of finding the Winners' enclosure.

Checklist

There are many things to consider when purchasing a racehorse, and this checklist is by no means comprehensive.

- Membership of ROA
- Weatherbys Bank Account
- Bloodstock agent or trainer for purchase
- Budget
- Trainer
- Type of horse
- Insurance
- Sponsorship
- Register for VAT
- Register colours
- Register a name

Syndicates, Racing Clubs and Charities

There are many racing clubs and syndicates, each offering a unique experience. It is a great way to enter the world of racehorse ownership, and you should choose the one that best fits your needs. Below is a list of some of the leading syndicates and clubs, but there are many more besides.

BG Racing Syndicates
https://bgracingsyndicates.co.uk/
Catch Us If You Can Racing
https://twitter.com/catchusracing
Craig Lidster Racing Club
https://www.craiglidsterracing.com/
David O'Meara Racing
https://www.davidomeararacing.com/ownership/syndicates
Habton Racing Club
https://www.habtonracingclub.com/
Hambleton Racing
https://www.hambletonracing.co.uk/
Hot To Trot Racing
https://hottotrotracing.com/
KVT Syndicates
https://www.kvtracing.com/
Making Headway Racing
https://www.makingheadwayracing.co.uk/
Middleham Park Racing
https://www.middlehamparkracing.net/
Nick Bradley Racing
https://nickbradleyracing.co.uk/
Ontoawinner
http://www.ontoawinner.net/

Ownaracehorse
https://www.ownaracehorse.co.uk/
Principle Racing
https://principleracing.com/
Racehorse Syndicates Association (RSA)
https://www.racehorsesyndicates.org/
Reality Syndicates
https://www.timeasterby.co.uk/syndicates/reality-syndicates
Santry Racing
https://twitter.com/RacingSantry
Stowe Racing Club
https://twitter.com/StoweRacing
Titanium Racing
http://www.titanium-racing.co.uk/
Ursa Major Racing
https://www.ursamajorracing.com/

Another good resource is the monthly "Inside The Rails" podcast promoting shared ownership.

If you would like more information on the Retraining Of Racehorses you can visit their website:-

https://www.ror.org.uk/

If you would like more information on the Injured Jockeys Fund you can visit their website:-

https://injuredjockeys.co.uk/ijf

About the author

Michael Madden has worked for many years in the IT industry, as a result of which he has been quoted in publications as prestigious as the *New York Times*. He continues to work around the globe, from Sao Paolo to Kiev and all places in between.

It was his involvement in IT that ultimately gave him the contacts and the understanding to get involved in the world of the thoroughbred.

He has self-published several books, including *Ole And Zac And The Port Of Tumbattle*, a rhyming picture book. In 2018 he released *The History Of Zombies*, a novel aimed at getting young teens off their electronic devices and into a book.

Michael has also had one book traditionally published, the authorised biography *Mike Sanchez Big Town Playboy*, for which he interviewed such legendary entertainers as Bill Wyman, Andy Fairweather Low, Albert Lee and Peter Richardson. The foreword was kindly provided by Robert Plant.

He is an avid blogger and occasional podcaster. Many of his podcasts are based on his interviews for various radio stations. The subjects include Suzi Quatro, Steve Harley, Carol Drinkwater, Wreckless Eric, Limahl, Marty Wilde, Right Said Fred and many more.

He has also performed as an after-dinner speaker on a number of occasions, as a result of another of his passions, playing amateur cricket.

In 2021 he became a racehorse owner, and he hopes to retain his ownerships for many years to come.

Originally from Sale in Cheshire, Michael now lives with his wife, Sally, in the more peaceful surroundings of Whaley Bridge, in the Peak District.

For information please visit:

http://michael-madden.co.uk/

Or follow on Twitter: @Tumbattle

Printed in Great Britain
by Amazon